Jean-Paul Jaccaud

62   De aedibus

Jean-Paul Jaccaud

Quart Verlag Luzern

Jean-Paul Jaccaud
62. Band der Reihe De aedibus / Volume 62 of the series De aedibus

Herausgeber / Edited by: Heinz Wirz, Luzern
Konzept/Concept: Heinz Wirz; Jean-Paul Jaccaud, Genf
Projektleitung / Project management: Quart Verlag, Linus Wirz
Textbeitrag / Article by: Irina Davidovici, Zürich
Objekttexte / Project descriptions: Jean-Paul Jaccaud
Vorwort/Foreword: Heinz Wirz
Textlektorat / Text editing: Miriam Seifert-Waibel, Hamburg
Übersetzung Französisch–Deutsch / French–German translation:
Christian Rochow, Berlin
Übersetzung Deutsch–Englisch / German–English translation: Benjamin Liebelt, Berlin
Fotos/Photos: Joël Tettamanti, Lausanne S./p. 8–33, 39, 42, 50–67, 70–71, 76–77, 86–87, 93; Hélène Binet, London S./p. 84, 89–91, 94–95, 97; David Grandorge, London S./p. 20, 31, 68, 73–75, 78–83, 96; Leo Fabrizio, Lausanne S./p. 34–37, 40–41; David Carlier, Aubonne S./p. 60–61; Fabio Galante, Genf S./p. 45–49
Künstlerische Leitung / Art direction: no-do / Noémie Gygax und/and Nicolas Leuba, Neuenburg
Grafische Umsetzung / Graphic design: Quart Verlag
Lithos: Printeria, Luzern
Druck/Printing: DZA Druckerei zu Altenburg GmbH

© Copyright 2016
Quart Verlag Luzern, Heinz Wirz
Alle Rechte vorbehalten / All rights reserved
ISBN 978-3-03761-116-6

Egalement publié en allemand–français / Ebenfalls publiziert
in Deutsch–Französisch (ISBN 978-3-03761-117-3)

Quart Verlag GmbH
Denkmalstrasse 2, CH-6006 Luzern
books@quart.ch, www.quart.ch

7	De aedibus 62 – Notat Heinz Wirz
9	Gemeinsame Projekte Jean-Paul Jaccaud im Gespräch mit Irina Davidovici Shared Projects Jean-Paul Jaccaud in conversation with Irina Davidovici
18	Sozialer Wohnungsbau mit Kinderkrippe, Rue du Cendrier, Genf Urban housing and crèche, Rue du Cendrier, Geneva
32	Haus G, Villa in Epalinges House G, Villa in Epalinges
40	Umwandlung eines Industriegebäudes in Saint-Jean, Genf Transformation of an industrial building in Saint-Jean, Geneva
48	Zwei Villen in Chambésy, Genf Two villas in Chambésy, Geneva
56	Chalet in/at La Forclaz, Evolène
66	Fassaden- und Wohnungssanierung, Le Lignon, Genf Façade and apartment renovation, Le Lignon, Geneva
76	Renovation eines Gebäudes an der Albert Street, London House renovation in Albert Street, London
82	Wohnanlage, Shepherdess Walk, London Housing in Shepherdess Walk, London
96	Wohnanlage, Sentier des Saules, Genf Housing block at the Sentier des Saules, Geneva
100	Wohnanlage, Eaux-Vives, Genf Housing block in Eaux-Vives, Geneva
106	Wohnanlage, Communaux d'Ambilly, Genf Housing block at the Communaux d'Ambilly, Geneva
110	Wohnanlage, Les Grottes, Genf Housing block in Les Grottes, Geneva
114	Werkverzeichnis / List of Works
116	Biografien, Mitarbeitende, Bibliografie, Dank Biographies, Team, Bibliography, Acknowledgements

De aedibus 62 – Notat
Heinz Wirz

In his *Scientific Autobiography*, Aldo Rossi almost casually states: "I have always stressed that locations are stronger than people; the location is stronger than events. That is the theoretical basis not only of my architecture, but architecture in general." The principle represents an idea by which the projects of the different architectural teams around Jean-Paul Jaccaud are primarily orientated. Through their designs, they seek to find a balance between the reference to the location and the city, the interweaving of buildings into the built environment, and the concrete conditions of the building's construction and programme. The latter two aspects are at the centre of a pragmatic approach that is enriched by the distillate of the reference to location and concept to form sophisticated solutions for major residential developments, administrative buildings and smaller houses, which are often developed into architectural gems with a poetic appearance and an integrative power.

Jean-Paul Jaccaud gathered his most important experience with Bernard Huet in Paris. He was an Intern for Huet, who was also his Diploma expert at the EPF Lausanne. It taught him to develop a keen eye for reading the city. Other stages in his career include the office of David Chipperfield in London and three years with the London office of Herzog & de Meuron.

The buildings in western Switzerland and London presented in this volume are however the product of teams with different protagonists and discussion partners. In Geneva, it is the office Jaccaud Spicher Architectes, where Jaccaud's partners include Lionel Spicher and Stephan Gratzer. The second office is in London, where designs are produced together with his wife and partner Tanya Zein Jaccaud. And finally several designs including the residential building with a crèche in Rue du Cendrier in Geneva were produced in cooperation with Sergison Bates architects in London and Zurich. In this way, a number of buildings of discreet beauty have been created in contrasting cultural environments, representing a far cry from the star culture surrounding certain individual architects and buildings, produced out of a passion for the city and the slow growth of the collective urban project.

Lucerne, October 2016

Jean-Paul Jaccaud, Stephan Gratzer,
Tanya Zein Jaccaud, Lionel Spicher

# Shared Projects
Jean-Paul Jaccaud in conversation
with Irina Davidovici

Coffee?

That would be nice.
We could start with your buildings, which belong to actual places and address at the same time archetypal conditions of city and landscape. This tension between general principles and particular situations covers the outline of an intellectual positioning. But you are not a stranger to working dialectically: during your studies at EPFL you were exposed to the 1990s Swiss discourse, with its known oscillations between abstraction and reference, concept and construction.

I was really young when I started studying architecture – about seventeen, so the first couple of years were more of a soft introduction. In my third year, I joined the studio of Bernard Huet, where I encountered an architectural culture and depth of knowledge that I found fascinating. For Huet everything was referential. He talked about memory and history, and would steer us through our sometimes naïve reiterations to help us understand where they could lead.

What kind of references did he use? High or low architecture?

Across the board, from contemporary to vernacular to gothic and classical – he saw the history of architecture as a continuum, but focused on readings of the city. I studied with Huet for three years, including my Diploma, then I went to Paris to work in his office for a year. I found his built work reflected the same encyclopedic knowledge. It was so dense that it often felt opaque, a little like reading Joyce. After a while I started to see architecture as inscribed in a long, slow process of city making, contributing to a much bigger whole, with different temporalities that it could not really influence. All this was a great contrast with what was happening in architecture at the time – even though the '90s were an interesting period in Switzerland.

So while Huet gave a very early foundation, providing contact with a very deep understanding, there was also a feeling there is also something else out there.

You formulated this as a tension between abstraction and reference. Building up the knowledge and the mechanisms of reference in a broader cultural context played an important part in my training. As for concepts, even then I was more aware of their limitations, certainly with respect to the city. There

London, 24 August 2015 and Zurich, 15 October 2015

9

Du sprachst von einer Bandbreite von Abstraktion zu Bezugnahme. Der Erwerb von Wissen, der Instrumente des Bezugs auf einen weiteren kulturellen Kontext spielte eine wichtige Rolle in meiner Ausbildung. Was Konzepte betrifft, so war ich mir schon damals ihrer Begrenztheit bewusst, ganz besonders hinsichtlich der Stadt. Es gab grosse Widerstände – ganz gewiss bei Huet – gegen Architektur als ein für sich bestehendes, künstlerisches, selbstbezügliches System. Diese Kritik zielte auf die Monumente des Modernismus, die sich jeweils als Solitär verstehen. Ich begriff, dass das Ergebnis solcher Prozesse auf grösserer, städtebaulicher Ebene einfach schrecklich ist. Konzepte müssen mit der Stadt in Einklang treten.

Gab es damals noch andere Einflüsse, die dich prägten?

Ich erinnere mich auch an die Lehrveranstaltungen von David Chipperfield, die aus anderen Gründen für mich interessant waren. Er kam gegen 1993 nach Lausanne und trug die Aura des Londoner Glamour an sich, erzählte Geschichten aus Japan und Harvard, zog sehr kultivierte und gewitzte Gäste wie Robert Maxwell hinzu. Er gab uns auf raffinierte, aber gleichzeitig freundliche und lustige Weise einen Einblick in den globalen Diskurs.

War das der Grund, warum du für Chipperfield in London gearbeitet hast?

Eine Woche nach meinem Diplomabschluss zog ich nach London, um in Chipperfields Büro zu arbeiten, wo ich bis 1998 blieb. Sein Büro befand sich damals in Agar Grove, das Team umfasste um die 18 Personen. Die Arbeitsbelastung war hoch, es war unglaublich anstrengend und auch die Nächte und die Wochenenden blieben nicht verschont, aber es war wundervoll. Von David lernte ich, dass man durchsetzungsfähig sein muss, und was das kostet. Manchmal musste er wirklich sehr energisch werden, damit etwas vorankam. Zu sehen, wie eine Position erwächst aus der Konfrontation mit Auftraggebern, Bauunternehmen und all den Kräften, die zersetzend auf die eigenen Überlegungen einwirken – so viel Engagement am Werk zu sehen, war prägend. Und die Auseinandersetzung mit dem Londoner Kulturleben war so bereichernd nach der Langeweile in Lausanne. Später wechselte ich [in das Londoner] Büro von Herzog & de Meuron und arbeitete am Laban Dance Centre mit. Dieses Büro hatte ich schon lange kennenlernen wollen, mich bewegte aber vor allem das Frühwerk von Herzog & de Meuron, während sie gewissermassen schon weitergezogen waren.

Heute ist deine Arbeit in ein Kooperationsnetz eingebunden, Kooperationen, die teils eher formaler, teils persönlicher Natur sind wie bei der Arbeit mit deiner

was a huge resistance – certainly with Huet – to architecture as a standalone, artistic, self-referential system. This critique could be linked back to the monumental pieces of modernism, each asserting itself individually. I understood that the result of such processes at the broader level of city making was blatantly painful. Concepts had to find a mediation within the city.

Were there other formative influences for you at the time?

I also recall David Chipperfield's teaching, which was interesting for other reasons. He came to Lausanne around 1993 with this aura of London glamour, with stories of Japan and of Harvard, bringing very cultured and witty guests like Robert Maxwell. He provided contact with a global discourse, sophisticated but at the same time warm and funny.

Is this how you came to work for Chipperfield in London?

The week after my Diploma I moved to London to work in Chipperfield's office, where I stayed until 1998. His studio was then in Agar Grove, a team of about eighteen people. The workload was intense and incredibly demanding, spilling into nights and weekends, but it was wonderful. From David I learned that you needed to be uncompromising and what it takes to do so. There were times when he really had to push for things to happen. Seeing a position emerging from confrontations with clients, builders, all the corrosive agents of one's thought: it was formative to see this level of commitment in action. And the exposure to London's cultural aspects was so enriching after the boredom of Lausanne. Later I moved to [the London office of] Herzog & de Meuron and worked on the Laban Dance Centre. Even though this was a practice I had long wanted to investigate, I projected on it what had interested me in their early work, and in a way they had already moved on.

Our shared experience at Herzog & de Meuron on the Laban Centre was shaped by the confrontation between imported design concepts on the one hand, and the realities of British construction on the other.

Intellectually, my experiences with Chipperfield and Herzog & de Meuron only confirmed the solidity of the bases acquired through Bernard Huet's teaching in Lausanne. But even though I felt a certain distance from Herzog & de Meuron's new direction, it was really difficult leaving the practice, suddenly finding myself without the intensity and kudos that came from working with them. I set up on my own practice straight after running a team of twenty-five on the Beijing Stadium competition, and found myself

Frau Tanya [Zein]. Es scheint dir zu gefallen, verschiedene Fertigkeiten und Fähigkeiten zusammenzubringen. Betrachtet ihr die Idee der Zusammenarbeit als eine formale, vertragliche Partnerschaft oder habt ihr dabei auch die wachsende heutige Tendenz zum kollektiven Schaffen, bis hin zu gemeinschaftlicher Urheberschaft, im Blick?

Ich wurde ein Einzelarchitekt, weil ich mich später selbstständig machte als die meisten Architekten meines Jahrgangs. Nachdem ich zehn Jahre im Ausland gearbeitet hatte, war bei meiner Rückkehr der Grossteil derjenigen, mit denen ich mir eine Zusammenarbeit hätte vorstellen können, schon andere Partnerschaften eingegangen. Ich habe immer eine diskursive Entwurfspraxis bevorzugt. Ich glaube, Projekte entwickeln sich durch Diskussionen, Mitteilung von Ideen, Fragen – in einem Prozess, der sich nicht aus sich heraus entwickelt, sondern aus der Auseinandersetzung mit anderen Vorstellungen. Dieses kollektive Projekt liegt implizit der Art zugrunde, wie Konzepte der Kritik offenstehen, bevor sie sich zu tief festgesetzt haben. Die Zusammenarbeit mit Sergison Bates in der Rue du Cendrier, die auf gemeinsamen Grundanschauungen beruhte, war insofern sehr bereichernd. Mit Tanya arbeite ich auf andere Weise zusammen: Sie unterzieht alles einer umfänglichen Kritik, was ich als sehr hilfreich empfinde. Wir streiten dabei viel und manchmal heftig, aber wenn das Projekt das übersteht, hat sich das wirklich gelohnt. Die Genfer Partnerschaft ist eine eher ergänzende Tätigkeit – wir tun ganz verschiedene Dinge. Lionel Spicher führt, managt und tut alles, damit das Projekt gebaut wird. Das sind Fertigkeiten, die mir fehlen.

Was unterscheidet aus deiner Sicht das Bauen in Grossbritannien vom Bauen in der Schweiz?

Es ist ein Kampf, aber wahrscheinlich kein schwierigerer als in der Schweiz. Wir empfanden die britischen Bauunternehmen als sehr kompetent, und in manchen Bereichen, so bei Metallbearbeitung und Maurerarbeit, ist das Know-how erstaunlich hoch. Zwar hielten Baukalkulatoren und Erschliesser unsere Arbeitsweise bei unserem Projekt in Shepherdess Walk für verrückt. Kulturell gab es die Erwartung, dass wir irgendein Metallgerüst hochziehen, es mit Schaumstoff verfüllen und Ziegel auf die Fassade klatschen – niemandem fiel etwas Besseres ein. Bei einem Projekt auf eigenes Risiko war der Einsatz von 45 Zentimeter starken Wänden mit Betonblöcken auf der Innenseite, zweischaligem Mauerwerk, Vollsteinen und Betonplatten eine Neuheit.

Beim Blick über deine Projekte zeigt sich eine Varianz von kleinen, privaten Aufträgen wie den Villen in Epalinges

in an empty room, missing all the action. In my work I aspired to find a middle way, in which both concept and reference could fit into a more collective project of city making. But it felt like a rather lonely endeavor at the time.

Nowadays you operate in a network of collaborations, some more formal, others the result of personal circumstance, such as working with your wife, Tanya. You seem comfortable with pooling together various skills and capabilities. Do you see the idea of collaboration as a formal contractual partnership, or are you exploring the growing tendency today to explore collectivity, in terms of authorship as well?

I became a sole practitioner through circumstance, because I set up on my own later than my contemporaries. After working abroad for ten years, when I came back most of those with whom I could have imagined working were already paired off. I have always preferred a discursive way of designing. I believe projects evolve through debate, sharing, questioning, a process that develops not from within, but from confrontation with other views. This collective project is implied in the way concepts stand up to critique before they are too deeply ingrained. The collaboration with Sergison Bates on rue du Cendrier, based on values we held in common, was very enriching. With Tanya [Zein] I work differently. She subjects everything to a barrage of critique, which I find helpful. We argue a lot, explosively at times, but if the project survives then it's worth holding to. The Geneva partnership is more complementary – we do very different things. Lionel Spicher runs, manages and does everything to ensure that the project gets built. These are skills I don't have.

What is your experience of building in the UK as opposed to Switzerland?

It is still a battle, but probably not more so than in Switzerland. We found British builders to be very competent and there is an amazing amount of know-how in certain trades, like metal work and bricklaying. Sure, quantity surveyors and developers thought it was crazy to build our project in Shepherdess Walk the way we did. Culturally there was the expectation that we put up some 'met sec', whack it full of foam, half-inch bricks on the front, and no one would be any wiser. For a speculative development it was pretty novel to build instead 45-centimeter walls, with block work on the inside and cavity walls, full bricks and concrete slabs.

The overview of your projects seems defined by the alternation of small, private commissions like the villas at Epalinges and Chambésy or the residential refurbishment

11

und Chambésy oder der Renovierung in Saint-Jean bis zu sehr urban bestimmten, stärker öffentlich wirkenden Gebäuden mit gemischter Nutzung.

Wir haben unser Interesse an kleinen Projekten bewahrt, weil sie ein vielfältiges Testfeld darstellen. Es ist hilfreich, im kleinen Massstab experimentell vorzugehen, die Atmosphäre und die Eigenart von Räumen zu testen. Hat man Materialien erst einmal von der Versuchswand genommen und in Oberflächen überführt, so sieht man, dass sie sich in den verschiedenen Belichtungssituationen und im Zusammenspiel mit anderen Materialien nie so verhalten, wie man es sich vorher gedacht hat. Die Idee, dass man alles auf Papier und mit Atelierversuchen planen könnte, erweist sich zunehmend als Irrtum. Auch der Massstabswechsel funktioniert nicht immer.

Bei kleinen Wohnprojekten musst du mit Auftraggebern arbeiten, die sehr klare persönliche Vorstellungen haben, die oftmals deinen eigenen zuwiderlaufen, während man bei grösseren Projekten spekulativer vorgehen kann, die Individualität dieser bestimmten Familie gegen die «Familie» in allgemeinen Sinn abwägen kann. Wie entwirfst du unter diesen verschiedenen Bedingungen?

Wenn wir wieder auf den Unterschied zwischen Bezugnahme und Konzept zurückgehen, so muss ich feststellen, dass die Menschen bei der Planung ihrer eigenen Häuser hautsächlich oder sogar ständig nur nach dem Konzept fragen. Anders als in Grossbritannien, wo der Status eines Hauses ein ganz anderer ist, hat beim Schweizer Konzept die Ausbreitung von einzigartigen Einfamilienhäusern eine verheerende Auswirkung auf die Landschaft. Ich finde die Produktion von einzigartigen Gebäuden, die alle auffallen wollen, entsetzlich geschmacklos. Das verkörpert einen Anspruch auf Konzept und Individualität auf Kosten eines gemeinschaftlichen Projekts. Deswegen versuchte ich bei der Villa in Epalinges die Forderungen des Auftraggebers in einem weiter gefassten Diskurs zu verankern, der Bezüge zur Landschaft aufnimmt, denn die unmittelbare gebaute Umgebung war, was Bezüge anbetraf, ausgesprochen armselig...

... weil es dort in der Umgebung nur Villen gibt.

Genau, und jede davon will anders sein. Ich versuchte, ein grösseres Organisationssystem zu finden, deswegen knüpfte ich den Entwurf an ein Merkmal der gesamten Region an. In der Gegend gibt es viele militärische Befestigungsanlagen, Bunker, die oft als Häuser verkleidet sind, bei denen Fenster auf den Beton gemalt sind. Diese getarnte Militärarchitektur bildete den stärksten Bezugspunkt und half, das Projekt von einer rein konzeptuellen Definition fernzuhalten. Das Projekt aus Beton mit

in Saint-Jean, with strongly urban buildings with a mix of programmes and more public in character.

We have retained an interest in small projects, because they offer a rich testing ground. It's helpful to be experimental at a small scale, in order to test the atmosphere and character of spaces. Once taken out from the sample panel and placed unto surfaces, in different light situations, confronted with each other, materials never do what you think they will. Increasingly the idea that you can plan everything on paper and studio samples turns out to be a fallacy. Even so, the transition between scales doesn't always work.

In small residential projects you have to work with clients who have their definite personal agenda, often at odds with your own, whereas in larger ones you can be more speculative, balance out the individuality of a family and the generality of 'the' family. How do you respond in design to these different conditions?

If we go back to the distinction between reference and concept, I find that when planning their own homes people tend to ask mostly, incessantly even, for concept alone. Unlike in Britain, where the status of the house is very different, in the Swiss context the sprawl of one-off family houses is having abysmal effects on the landscape. I find the production of unique pieces, urging to stand out, totally distasteful. It epitomises the demands of concept and individuality versus a more collective project. So for the villa at Epalinges I tried to anchor the client's requirements in a broader discourse, drawing references from the landscape, since the immediate built environment was, referentially speaking, rather poor.

... As there are only other villas around.

Precisely, and each one is vying to be different. I tried identifying a broader organising system, so I linked the design to a characteristic of the wider region. The area is dotted with military fortifications, bunkers often dressed up as houses, with windows painted on the concrete. This concealed military architecture was the strongest point of reference and helped steer the project away from a purely conceptual definition. Built in concrete with small windows, the project was quickly known in the neighbourhood as the 'bunker', which I was entirely happy with.

The symmetrical villas at Chambesy stand out in their relation between singularity and duality – almost as if you are saying, we are all identical in our desire to be unique. What was the nature of the commission? They are called villas, but in essence they are two semi-detached houses.

seinen kleinen Fenstern wurde in der Nachbarschaft schnell als der «Bunker» bekannt, und damit war ich absolut zufrieden.

Bei deinen Genfer Projekten ergibt die gleiche eingehende Würdigung des Kontexts ganz andere Resultate. Einerseits ist die formale Sprache so kontrolliert, dass sie fast automatisch einen allgemeinen Zustand ausdrückt. Das wiederum macht die Gebäude typisch städtisch. Andererseits aber findest du viele Gründe, die Gebäude nicht symmetrisch zu machen, will sagen: Jede Formentscheidung ergibt sich aus einer Lektüre der Bedingungen des Baugeländes oder aus programmatischen Anforderungen. Wäre die Mutmassung richtig, dass deine Architektur in erster Linie als eine Reihe von Reaktionen entsteht? Ist diese Offenheit deine Ausgangsposition?

Es stimmt, in jedem Fall spielt das Baugelände eine definierende Rolle, und bei den meisten Projekten entwickelt sich die Form aus den Qualitäten der Umgebung. Die Gestalt entsteht aus einer Reihe pragmatischer Reaktionen auf den jeweiligen Kontext, darum unterscheiden sich die Projekte im Ergebnis. Am Ende sind wir von der Gestalt, die die Gebäude letztlich annehmen, selbst überrascht – ein formales [oder stilistisches] Apriori gibt es wirklich überhaupt nicht.

Gleichwohl gehst du von einem typologischen Gesichtspunkt aus, der sich auf allgemeine städtebauliche Bedingungen bezieht: die Strassenfront, eine gewisse Regelmässigkeit bei den Öffnungen...

Wir schätzen gattungstypische Qualitäten wegen ihres kulturellen Gehalts. Dennoch entwickeln wir letztlich unsere Projekte aus ihren interessanten, komplexen, nicht immer kohärenten städtischen Umgebungen heraus oder schälen sie aus ihnen heraus. Wir hatten das Glück, dass die meisten Projekte sich in solchen spezifischen Ortslagen befanden, denn unter diesen Bedingungen gelingen uns die erfolgreichsten Entwürfe.

Das ist eine Architektur der kleinen Gesten, die sich gewissermassen in das Gelände hineinwebt oder -strickt.

Wohl wahr, aber dieses Hineinstricken kann auf ganz verschiedene Art geschehen. Bei Les Grottes zum Beispiel schrieb das unregelmässige, dreieckige Grundstück ein Gebäude vor, das so kompakt und so hoch wie möglich sein musste. Damit setzten wir uns von der Lage inmitten einer sehr präzisen geschlossenen Blockbebauung ab. Das Projekt reagiert auf weiter entfernte Anknüpfungspunkte – den Park und die grösseren Gebäude –, aber nicht auf das gleichmässige städtische Gefüge in seiner unmittelbaren Umgebung. Während wir bei einigen Projekten die Blockrandbebauung und das bestehende Gefüge komplettierten, verhält sich dieses

There was something disturbing about bringing into this established residential neighbourhood the smaller scale of the semi-detached houses; it felt completely at odds with its context. From very early on we envisaged a certain size and presence to the massing of the building so as to better address its surrounds, integrate it into the rhythm and scale of its neighbours. The rental programme, on the other hand, called for two identical units. We tried to assert the individuality of each at the back of the site, but on the street they merge into a single ordering whole, which can be perceived as one house. In order to retain a larger shared garden at the back, we articulated the built volumes so as to mark two private territories facing away from each other.

What I'm trying to say is that the symmetry did not arise out of a formal desire or conceptual exploration. In fact, internally the geometry breaks up a lot. On the outside however, I just could not find a good enough reason not to make the houses symmetrical. At the back you don't even perceive them as such, you can never step back far enough. By contrast, the front is strongly axial and slightly pompous. It was intentionally quite an ironic interpretation of the upmarket, self-gratifying neighbourhood.

The same close appraisal of context gives, in your Geneva projects, very different results. On the one hand, the formal language is so controlled as to express almost by default a general condition. In turn this renders the buildings intrinsically urban. On the other hand you find plenty of reasons not to make them symmetrical, so to speak: every formal decision results from a reading of site circumstances or programmatic demands. Would it be correct to surmise that your architecture is determined primarily as a series of responses? Is this openness your priori position?

True, in every case the site plays a defining role, and most projects develop formally from the qualities of their environment. Shapes develop from a series of pragmatic responses to each context, so every project is different as a result. We end up being surprised by the shapes buildings are ultimately taking – there is really no formal [or stylistic] a priori in anything.

You start nevertheless from a typological reading, which is dealing with the generality of city conditions: the street frontage, a certain regularity in openings...

We celebrate generic qualities for their cultural content. Still, ultimately we "extract" or untangle our projects from their interesting, complex, not always coherent urban environments. We have been lucky in that most projects have been located

Gebäude nicht mimetisch zum Gefüge. Vielmehr verknüpft es sich mit seiner unmittelbaren Umgebung durch die fliessende Bewegung, die es auf dem Gelände erschafft, indem öffentliche Fusswege rund um die kompakte Grundfläche des Gebäudes angelegt wurden.

Im Gegensatz dazu wirkt der weit geschwungene Bogen der Gebäude von Gourgas-Maraîchers wie eine eher monumentale Geste.

Die Form, die hier entstanden ist, ist tatsächlich das Ergebnis von präzisen Erkundungen der städtebaulichen Situation. Dieser Stadtteil ist von langen, schmalen Gebäuden bestimmt und erfordert eine hohe Verdichtung. Die Gebäude in der Rue de Maraîchers sind zwar bunt zusammengewürfelt, beachten aber alle den starken 30-Meter-Rhythmus. Wir mussten mit dieser städtebaulichen Bedingung der langen Gebäuderiegel zurechtkommen, wollten aber verhindern, dass sich zwei davon gegenüberstanden und sich gegenseitig verschatteten. Wir nutzten den vorhandenen Rhythmus der Strasse, führten aber ein Ende unseres Gebäudes um die Ecke, sodass eine Reihe der Wohnungen auf den Park an der entgegengesetzten Ecke blickt. Die abgestufte Biegung hinten lenkt den Blick von den Balkonen und aus den Wohnzimmern fort von den gegenüberliegenden Gebäuden in Längsrichtung nach Westen. Durch diese Orientierung wird eine freie Sichtlinie von 150 Metern statt von 10 oder 15 Metern erzielt. Was wie eine hochgradig formbestimmte Lösung aussieht, entstand tatsächlich aus einer Reihe pragmatischer Reaktionen auf die Bedingungen des Kontextes. Eine komplexe offene Typologie verbessert die Lebensqualität in diesem schwierigen räumlichen Umfeld. Wir sind immer wieder überrascht, wohin uns unsere pragmatischen Schritte schliesslich führen.

Was tust du, wenn solche unmittelbaren oder ferneren Bezüge fehlen? Der Kontext der Erschliessung in Ambilly ist beispielsweise eher nichtssagend.

Das Baugrundstück ist ein Kartoffelacker! Hier entwickelte sich das Projekt aus dem Charakter der Bauaufgabe. Die Auftragsvergabe erfolgte über Gespräche mit den Konkurrenten und entwickelte sich über eine Reihe von Diskussionen in der Zusammenarbeit von vier Architekturbüros. Wir arbeiteten mit Pierre und Mireille Bonnet, BassiCarella und LRS architectes zusammen, um eine alle Gebäude übergreifende Konsistenz zu erzielen, eine Art Anti-Autonomie, die den wirklichen Eindruck eines Ensembles vermittelt. In Workshops entwickelten wir ein Register gemeinsamer Elemente. Die Landschaft ist sehr flach, deswegen betonten wir im Fassadenaufbau die Horizontale, und die Gebäude gehen darauf unterschiedlich ein. Wir

in such particular situations, and it is in relation to these that we come up with the most successful schemes.

It's an architecture of small gestures, like weaving or stitching into the site.

Indeed, but stitching can occur in different ways. For example, at Les Grottes the odd triangular site dictated a building as compact and as tall as possible. In that, we went against its location among very precise perimeter blocks. The project responds to the more distant conditions of the park and larger-scale buildings further away, rather than the consistent urban fabric immediately around it. While in some projects we complete perimeter blocks and try to complement the existing fabric, this building doesn't respond mimetically to it. Rather, it stitches to its immediate situation through the fluidity of movement it generates across the site, by integrating public pathways around its compact footprint.

By contrast, the sweeping arch of the Gourgas-Maraîchers building looks like a rather grand gesture.

The form it took is in fact the outcome of precise readings of its situation. This part of the city has a fabric of long, narrow buildings, with very high density requirements. The buildings on rue de Maraîchers are very eclectic but all have the same strong rhythm of 30 metres. We needed to deal with this urban condition of long bar buildings, but at the same time wanted to avoid having two of them facing and overshadowing each other. We used the existing pace of the street, but we angled one end of our building so that a number of flats look towards the park on the opposite corner. The stepped curvature at the back guides the view from balconies and living rooms away from the facing building, and re-orients it lengthways, facing west. This orientation gives a clear view of 150 metres instead of 10 or 15. So what looks like a highly formal solution is actually generated by a series of pragmatic responses to site conditions. A complex typology of openness improves the quality of life in this difficult urban condition. We are always surprised to see what we arrive at, following through a series of pragmatic steps.

What do you do when these immediate or more distant references are missing? The context of the Ambilly development, for example, is more muted.

The site is a potato field! Here, the project emerged from the nature of the commission. It was commissioned through competitive interviews, and as a collaboration between four architectural practices it evolved through a lot of discussions. With Pierre and Mireille Bonnet, BassiCarella and LRS architects

bestimmten eine begrenzte Materialpalette aus rund 20 verschiedenen Sorten Beton und zehn verschiedenen Verputzarten. Durch diese Eingrenzung der Möglichkeiten ergibt sich eine Ähnlichkeit von Farbtönen und Materialien, obwohl die Gebäude selbst sehr unterschiedlich sind. Wenn man ein begrenztes Vokabular verwendet, wie das in der Stadt des 19. Jahrhunderts der Fall war, geht weniger schief. Der gewählte Ansatz ermöglicht Verschiedenheit, sorgt aber auch für eine Anbindung jedes einzelnen Projekts an das umfassende organisatorische System. Im Ergebnis hat die Erschliessung einen ausgeprägt städtischen Charakter, obschon die Umgebung derart beliebig ist.

Und dieser Charakter ist bewusst gewählt. Es ist interessant, wie beim Fehlen von Besonderheiten allgemeinere Bedingungen des Städtebaus ins Spiel kommen. Richtet sich deine Arbeit auf das Ziel einer universellen Urbanität? Oder ist dein Ansatz in spezifischeren Stadtcharakteren verankert, etwa dem von Genf oder London?

Erst einmal versuchen wir, die Bedingungen zu verstehen, aus denen ein spezifischer Charakter entstanden ist. Darauf folgt eine kreativere Phase der Deutung. In diesem Fall interessierte uns das Verhältnis zwischen den Standards des sozialen Wohnungsbaus und der Stadtplanung als Ursprung einer bestimmten Standardisierung. Seit den 1960er Jahren bezieht sich ein grosser Teil des sozialen Wohnungsbaus in Genf auf den Plan localisé du quartier, eine mittlere Stufe der Stadtplanung, die zwischen dem kantonalen Plan directeur und der Ebene des bebauten Blocks angesiedelt ist. Darin sind einige Schlüsseldimensionen, Höhe, Tiefe, Zahl der Geschosse und so weiter, festgelegt. Als Ergebnis eines modernistischen, fast reflexhaften Agierens führten die Planer systematisch Blocks von 15 mal 50 Metern ein. Diese etablierte Lösung wird als ökonomisch wünschenswert begriffen, führt aber im Ergebnis zur Wiederholung von begrenzten, typologisch schlechten Konfigurationen, die im negativen Sinne gattungstypisch sind. Urbanistisch gesehen, ist diese Lösung ebenfalls unbefriedigend, weil sie die Probleme, die der Modernismus mit der Gestaltung geschlossener Strassenfronten hatte, deutlich hervortreten lässt.
Bei diesen 15-Meter-Blocks erzeugt der heutige Gebäudestandard in der Regel eine Abfolge kleiner Treppenhäuser mit jeweils zwei oder drei Wohnungen pro Geschoss. Die meisten Wohnungen sind in zwei Richtungen orientiert und haben eine tiefen Grundriss, sodass es im mittleren Bereich fast immer zu dunkel ist. Die Erfahrung hat uns gelehrt, dass man dieser typischen Bedingung dadurch entgegenwirken kann, dass so viele Ecksituationen wie möglich geschaffen werden. Deswegen haben wir auch das Gebäude in Ambilly über den vier untersten Stockwerken aufgebrochen. Dahinter steckt ein bestimmtes Grundprinzip: Ecken erweisen sich

we worked together to establish a consistency across all buildings, a sense of anti-autonomy which gives the real sense of an ensemble. Through workshops we developed a register of common elements. The landscape is very flat, so we emphasized horizontality in the composition of elevations, and the buildings open up to it in different ways. We established a limited material palette of about twenty different concretes and ten different renders, narrowing down the possibilities, so that there is a tonal and material similarity even though the buildings are very different. Employing a limited vocabulary, like in the nineteenth-century city, means that fewer things can go wrong. This approach has allowed diversity, but also a mediation between each project and the broader organisational system. As a result, despite its indeterminate surrounds, the development is essentially urban.

And deliberately so. It's interesting to see how in the absence of particulars, more generic conditions of city-making have come into play. Do you pursue in your work a universal urbanity? Or is your approach anchored into more specific urban characters, such as that of Geneva, or London?

In the first place we try to understand the conditions that have given rise to a generic character. This is followed by a more creative, interpretative stage. In this case, we were interested in the relation between social housing standards and city planning as the origin of a certain standardisation. Much of Geneva's social housing from the 60s onwards departs from the Plan localisé du quartier, an intermediate scale of urban planning that mediates between the cantonal Plan directeur and the scale of perimeter blocks, giving a few key dimensions, height, width, number of floors and so forth. As the result of a modernist, almost reflex action, the planners systematically implement 15 by 50-metre blocks. This established solution is understood to be economically desirable, but the result is a repetition of limited, typologically poor configurations – generic in a negative sense. It is also unsatisfactory from an urban point of view, because it propagates the modernist difficulty to generate consistent street frontages.
In these 15-metre blocks, the current housing standards typically generate a succession of small stairwells, each with two or three flats on each level. Most apartments have a double orientation and end up with a deep plan, which is almost always too dark in the middle. We found through experience that this generic condition can be counteracted by generating as many corner conditions as possible, which is also why we have broken up the Ambilly building above the first four floors. There is a certain rationale behind it: corners help with the surface constraints for social housing, and the

angesichts der begrenzten Fläche im sozialen Wohnungsbau als nützlich, und die räumliche Organisation wird effizienter. Bei gleicher Flächenanforderung können wir so fünf bis sechs Wohnungen pro Geschoss unterbringen, für grosszügigere Eingangsbereiche und freien Ausblick sorgen. In Ambilly waren wir die einzigen, die Eckblocks verwendeten, aber auch die einzigen, die sich mit einem stark regulierten Gehalt auseinandersetzen mussten. Ohne die räumlichen Beschränkungen des sozialen Wohnungsbaustandards lassen sich sehr schöne Wohnungen in allen möglichen Konfigurationen errichten, auch in Zeilenbebauung.

Deine Untersuchung der Ecklage stellt eine Kritik dar: Du bestimmst die Grenzen der konventionellen Lösungen und findest gleichzeitig andere Mittel, mit denen du operierst.

Von Beginn an haben wir reflexhaftes Handeln und kulturelle Hintergründe, die vom Modernismus ererbt sind, bekämpft. Obwohl es sehr schöne Viertel gibt, etwa Champel, das auf den Braillard-Plan zurückgeht, ist Genfs Besessenheit von Wohnanlagen, die dem Riegelprinzip folgen, augenfällig. Obwohl Braillards eigene, hervorragende Gebäude selten Zeilenbauten sind, vererbte sich der Reflex über die Generationen – sowohl Le Corbusier als auch Saugey griffen darauf zurück. Kulturell gesehen sind die Planungen, die gegenwärtig für Städte angestellt werden, das Ergebnis einer langen Kette weitergegebener Verfahrensweisen. Und oft fehlt den Planern die Einsicht, sie zu interpretieren oder Weiterentwicklungen zu ermöglichen. Wir streben nach interessanteren Wegen der Begegnung, wollen Möglichkeiten für zeitgemässe Regulierungen eröffnen. In unserer Arbeit versuchen wir, Planungsbeschränkungen zu umgehen und arbeiten zunehmend mit 20, 25, 30 Meter tiefen Blocks. Wir entdeckten, dass Ecklösungen ein ganzes neues Register von Möglichkeiten eröffnen.
Je mehr wir bauen, umso stärker entwickeln wir aus gänzlich pragmatischen Überlegungen heraus ein Formenvokabular. In Genf ist die Qualität des städtischen Gefüges oft das Resultat direkter Reaktionen auf Einschränkungen durch Stadtplanung oder Bauvorschriften. Oft verzweigt sich ein intelligenter, urbaner Vorschlag dann zu einem nutzbaren Vokabular.

Der Riegel-Reflex führt auf die Begrenztheit von Konzepten zurück – man braucht mehr als nur eine einzelne Idee, um ein Projekt durchzuführen. Dein Ansatz entwickelt sich aus dem systematischen Umgang mit gegebenen Bedingungen. Du verwirfst diese Bedingungen nicht, akzeptierst sie aber auch nicht. Du arbeitest innerhalb der existierenden Parameter und versuchst, bestehende, konventionelle Lösungen zu verbessern: nicht weil diese konventionell, sondern weil sie problematisch sind.

spatial organization is more efficient. With the same capacity ratio we can bring five or six flats per floor, provide generous entrance spaces and open views. In Ambilly we were the only ones to use corner blocks, but also the only ones dealing with a heavily regulated content. Without the spatial constraints of social housing standards one can do very nice housing in all sort of configurations, including bar developments.

Your search for corner conditions represents a critique: you identify the limitations of conventional solutions and at the same time find a different set of tools to operate with.

From the start we have been fighting reflex actions and cultural backgrounds inherited from modernism. Although there are very nice areas built like that, like Champel, going back to the Braillard plan, Geneva's obsession with bar-shaped housing is still very prominent. Even though Braillard's own, extraordinary buildings are rarely "Zeilenbau", the reflex has been carried though generations – both Le Corbusier and Saugey used it. Culturally speaking, the urban plans currently being drawn up are the result of a long chain of handed-down ways of doing things. Often planners haven't yet got the insight to interpret it or make it evolve. We look for more interesting ways to meet and open up possibilities for contemporary regulations. In our work we have tended to go around planning constraints and to work increasingly with 20, 25, 30 metre-deep blocks. We found that corner conditions open a whole new register of possibilities.
The more we build, the more we develop a formal vocabulary from entirely pragmatic considerations. In Geneva, the quality of urban fabric is often the result of direct responses to urban planning and regulatory constraints. Once an intelligent urban proposal is found, it often branches off into vocabulary that can then be used.

The bar-reflex goes back to the limitation of concepts – you need more than an individual idea in order to carry a project through. Your approach develops from systematically dealing with given conditions. You don't reject them, but you don't accept them either. You work within the given parameters and try to improve on existing, conventional solutions: not because they are conventional, but because they are problematic.

Good architecture often attacks convention but very consciously so. Once you completely remove the notion of convention, even the driest possible kind, rather than confronting it, then you step back into arbitrariness.

Some people avoid arbitrariness by defining a concept in isolation of external conditions and holding on to that

Gute Architektur greift häufig Konventionen an, aber sie tut das sehr bewusst. Sobald man den Begriff der Konvention, und wenn es sich um die langweiligsten handelt, einfach ausblendet, statt sich ihm zu stellen, fällt man in Beliebigkeit zurück.

Manche Leute vermeiden Beliebigkeit, indem sie ein Konzept ohne jede Berücksichtigung äusserer Bedingungen definieren und an diesem als einem orientierungsstiftenden, ordnenden Mittel im Entwurfsprozess festhalten. Aber Konzepte bleiben immer selbst auferlegte Ordnungen. Ich empfinde deine Art, mithilfe des Plans zu denken, als in einer Weise stringent, die in Diskussionen über Architektur nicht häufig zu finden ist, jedenfalls nicht explizit. Bei Diskussionen geht es häufig um die grossen Ideen, das Definieren von Positionen und die Rechtfertigung ihrer Einzigartigkeit. Was kann man aber heute tun, wenn das Inventar der Möglichkeiten von der früheren Generation der Architekten so gründlich ausgeschöpft wurde? Das einfach ignorieren und sich auf den Common Sense zurückziehen, auf die kleinen Gesten, die gute Architektur schaffen?

Grosse Gesten sind in der Regel auf Individualität, Isolierung und Exklusivität im schlechten Sinne ausgerichtet. Ist dir aufgefallen, wie oft das Wort «exklusiv» verwendet wird, und immer als etwas Wünschenswertes? Ich verstehe einen exklusiven Ort als einen Ort, der exkludiert, also ausschliesst. Elitäres Denken ist in einer bestimmten Art von Architektur, die alles beiseiteschieben und jedes Gebäude zu einem einmaligen Werk machen möchte, sehr ausgeprägt. Ich hingegen glaube, dass es so etwas wie ein Gemeinschaftsprojekt gibt, bei dem es nicht um einzelne Werke, sondern um die Einfügung in verschiedene Zeiträume, in weiter gefasste Ordnungssysteme geht. Als Architekten können wir unsere Verantwortlichkeit für diese gemeinsamen Aspekte unserer Arbeit nicht ignorieren.

as an orienting, ordering device in the design process. But concepts remain a self-imposed discipline. I find the way you think through the plan compelling in a way that doesn't so often occur in discussions about architecture, not explicitly at least. Discussions are often about the big ideas, defining positions and justifying their uniqueness. But when this array of possibilities has been so thoroughly exhausted by the previous generation of architects, what can you do now? Just ignore it and go back to common sense, to the small gestures that make good architecture?

Big gestures tend to be about individuality, isolation and exclusiveness, in the negative sense of the word. Have you noticed how you hear the word "exclusive", not only all the time, but also as something desirable? I understand an exclusive place as a place that excludes. Elitism is very strong in a certain kind of architecture which is all about brushing everything aside, making each piece unique. On the contrary, I believe there is such a notion as a common project, which is not about individual pieces but about fitting into different timescales, into broader organising systems. As architects we cannot ignore our responsibility for these shared aspects of our work.

Sozialer Wohnungsbau mit Kinderkrippe, Rue du Cendrier, Genf

Das Projekt für ein Gebäude des sozialen Wohnungsbaus und eine Kindertagesstätte in der Genfer Rue du Cendrier befindet sich an der Gelenkstelle zwischen dem modernistischen städtischen Gefüge des Centre Mont Blanc von Marc-Joseph Saugey und der Strassenlandschaft der Rue Rousseau aus dem 18. Jahrhundert. Das Gebäude vermittelt zwischen diesen beiden Situationen durch eine Volumetrie, die sowohl die Massstäblichkeit der Parzellengliederung des 18. Jahrhunderts in der Rue Rousseau aufgreift als auch die Sockelfigur des Centre Mont Blanc in der Rue du Cendrier fortsetzt. Durch die subtile Krümmung der Fassadenelemente wird das Projekt ein Mal als Verlängerung der Strassenfront wahrgenommen, während das andere Mal die Figur des Sockels und des von diesem abgesetzten Volumens ins Auge fällt.

Die Organisation der Zugangswege zu den Wohnungen als offene Laubengänge stellt einen spezifischen Bezug zur Morphologie des Hofs im historischen Viertel von St. Gervais her, von dem das Gebäude auch die Figur der Toreinfahrt übernimmt. Die Fassaden aus vorgefertigtem Beton vermitteln zwischen den Vorhangfassaden des Centre Mont Blanc von Saugey und dem Mauerwerk in der Rue Rousseau.

Urban Housing and crèche, Rue du Cendrier, Geneva

The project for social housing and a crèche at the Rue du Cendrier in Geneva is located at the articulation between the modernist urban fabric of the Centre Mont Blanc by Marc Saugey and the 18th century streetscape of the rue Rousseau. The building mediates between these two conditions by a volume that retains the rhythm of the 18th century frontages on the rue Rousseau and simultaneously prolongs the plinth condition on the Marc Saugey buildings. Through a subtle folding of the façade elements the project is perceived in changing ways from different viewpoints, either as a continuous street frontage or a plinth with a superior volume.

The organisation of the circulation and distribution spaces as an open walkway refers specifically to the morphology of the St. Gervais area, also visible in the large "porte cochère" type doorway opening onto the street. The façades of the building, in prefabricated concrete, attempt a further mediation between the curtain walling of the Mont Blanc Centre and the fine masonry work of the rue Rousseau.

Jaccaud Spicher Architectes mit/with Sergison Bates architects
Wettbewerb/Competition: 2006
Bauzeit/Construction: 2009–2011
Bauherr/Client: Ville de Genève, FVGLS
Team: Jean-Paul Jaccaud, Jonathan Sergison, Stephen Bates, Lionel Spicher, Federico Dos Santos, Steffen Jürgensen, Christophe Neyroud, Silvia Palhao
Fachplaner/Consultants: Sancha SA, R. Moser SA, MAB ing. SA, Schumacher SA, AcouConsult Sàrl

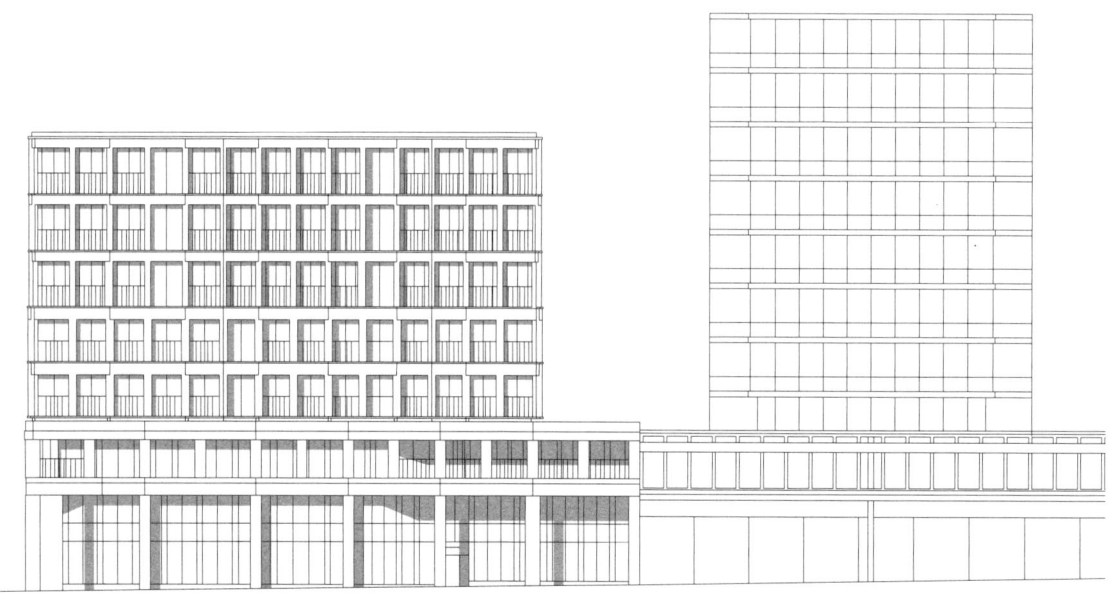

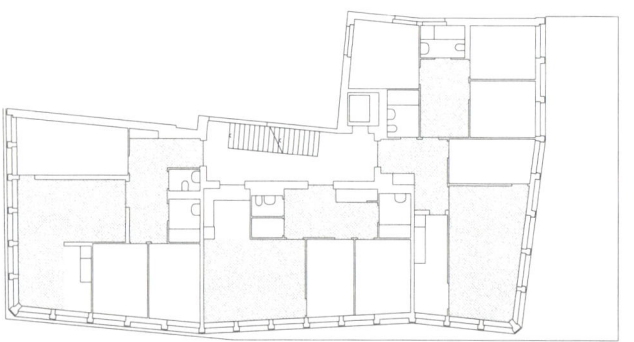
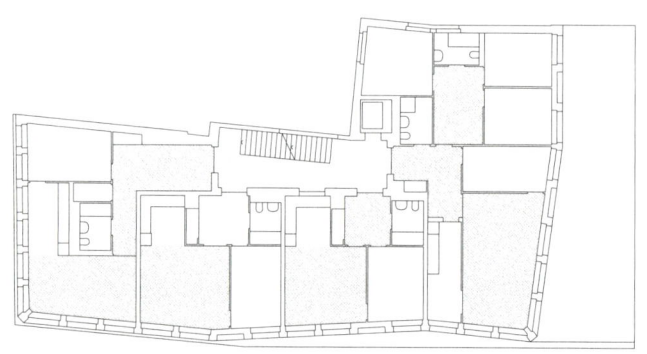

Haus G, Villa in Epalinges

House G, Villa in Epalinges

Haus G befindet sich auf einem schmalen Grundstück mit einem sehr starken Gefälle in Südwest-Richtung. Das Volumen beschreibt eine fortgesetzte Krümmung, um die Hauptwohnbereiche nach Süden auszurichten. Die daraus resultierende Silhouette gibt dem Baukörper den Charakter einer grob zugehauenen Skulptur und verweist auf die Formensprache der Bunker, die in dieser Landschaft sehr präsent ist. Der Eindruck, einem facettenreichen Gebäude gegenüberzustehen, wird noch durch das Dach verstärkt, dessen vier Seiten sich jeweils ungleichmässig abzeichnen, der Konfiguration der Umfassungsmauern entsprechend.

Die Annäherung an das Gebäude erfolgt über eine Terrasse, von der aus man nur den oberen Teil des Gebäudes und die Eingangstür wahrnimmt. Von hier aus wirkt das Gebäude klein. Vom Eingangsbereich aus leiten Fenster, die sich zum Garten hin öffnen, den Weg zum Wohnzimmer. Dieses grosse Zimmer, dessen Präsenz die Gesamtvolumetrie im Vorhinein nicht erahnen lässt, scheint inmitten der Bäume zu schweben – das grosse Glasfenster gibt den Blick auf die abstrakte, sich ständig verändernde Komposition des Blätterwerks frei. Die innere Gipsverkleidung ist eingefaltet, um einen Eindruck von Leichtigkeit zu vermitteln; sie erinnert an Schinkels Zeltzimmer oder an die Dünnwandigkeit einer Zeltplane.

The House G is situated at Epalinges in the canton of Vaud. The very narrow plot faces on to the "Bois de Ban" forest below with a very steep diagonal slope on a South-West orientation. The project attempts to optimise the land use and the sun exposure with a folded volume that reconciles the geometry of the road at the top of the site with the orientation of the slope below.

The narrowness of the site and the lack of possibility of standing back from the house led to a folded volume whose proportions and character change constantly, with deep revealed windows framing the varied views of the landscape. The building appears very small from the top of the site, with only a front door visible. As one progresses internally however the main circulation leads progressively to the living area, a large space not perceivable from the entrance, which appears to hover over the forest below at an uncertain height. A large horizontal window opens on to the living area, framing only the foliage of the trees as an abstract backdrop to everyday life.

If the building's external character and materiality hint at the military bunker architecture that is very present in the area, the interior is given a lightness and textile-like quality by faceted plasterboard, recalling perhaps a tent, or the "Zeltzimmer" so dear to classical German architects.

Jean-Paul Jaccaud Architectes mit/with DPX Architectes
Bauzeit/Construction: 2004–2007
Bauherr/Client: privat/private
Team: Jean-Paul Jaccaud, Lionel Spicher, Grégoire Dupasquier, François de Marignac, Gregor Kamplade
Fachplaner/Consultants: Sancha SA

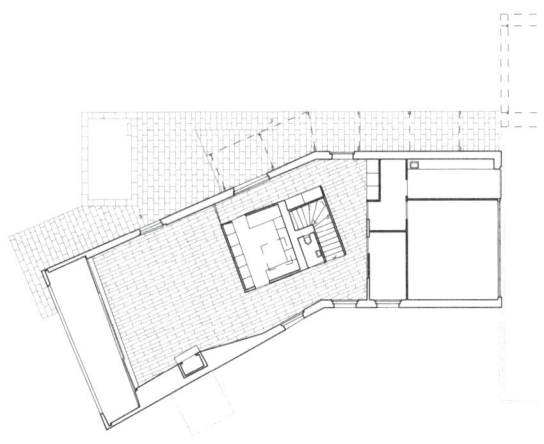
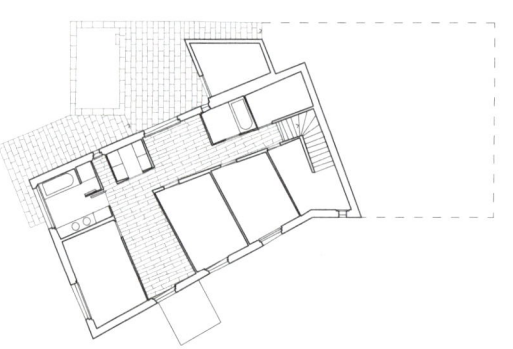

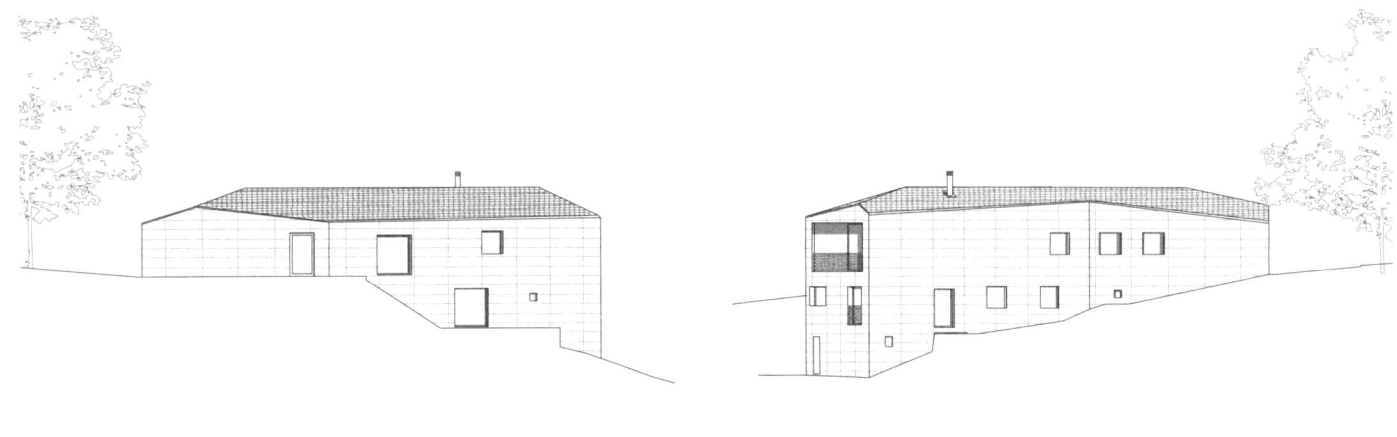

Umwandlung eines Industriegebäudes in Saint-Jean, Genf

Transformation of an industrial building in Saint-Jean, Geneva

Ein altes Werksgebäude in malerischer Lage nahe dem Ufer der Rhône im Genfer Zentrum wurde in eine gemischte Nutzung (Büros und Wohnungen) umgewandelt. Die Büros liegen auf der unteren Ebene und werden von oben durch zwei grosse Lichtschächte, die vom Dach aus das Gebäude durchschneiden, belichtet. Diese tiefen Öffnungen aus unverkleidetem Sichtbeton spiegeln den Charakter des Industriebaus wider und ermöglichen einen Durchblick in den Himmel. Die obere, dem Wohnen vorbehaltene Etage ist um grosse, durchgehende Wohnbereiche organisiert, die durch neue Öffnungen im Dach und an der Fassade in die bestehende Gebäudekonstruktion eingefügt sind. Der ursprüngliche Gewerbecharakter der Stätte zeigt sich sowohl in der grosszügigen Räumlichkeit der Eingriffe als auch in der Wahl der Materialien.

Die Fassade aufseiten der Rhône ist eine Neuinterpretation der ursprünglichen, bei der der abgehackte Rhythmus der bestehenden Öffnungen durch neue von ähnlichen Proportionen ergänzt wurde. Die dunklen Töne des Verputzes integrieren das Gebäude in die umgebende Vegetation und bilden einen Kontrast zu den hellen Fassaden der benachbarten Wohnbebauung.

A disused industrial building located in an idyllic setting adjacent to the River Rhône in the centre of Geneva was transformed with a mixed programme of housing and office space. The offices located at the lower level are partially top-lit by two large light wells that cut through the building from the roof level. These deep openings in rough concrete are in keeping with the industrial character of the building and allow for glimpses of sky from the lower floor. The top floor apartment is organised around very generous living and dining room spaces that are also open to the sky through a series of rough concrete rooflights. These rooflights and the new opening on the façades stitch the new project into the existing building to form a complex whole where the old is difficult to distinguish from the new.

The façade on the River Rhône is a reinterpretation of the original that completes the syncopated composition with additional openings of similar proportion. The dark colouring of the render integrate the building into the dense vegetation that surrounds it in contrast with the light tones of the neighbouring housing block.

Jaccaud Spicher Architectes
Bauzeit/Construction: 2012–2014
Bauherr/Client: Privat/private
Team: Jean-Paul Jaccaud, Lionel Spicher, Jonas Altorfer, Manon Gerardy, Hildur Ýr Ottósdóttir
Fachplaner/Consultants: EDMS SA

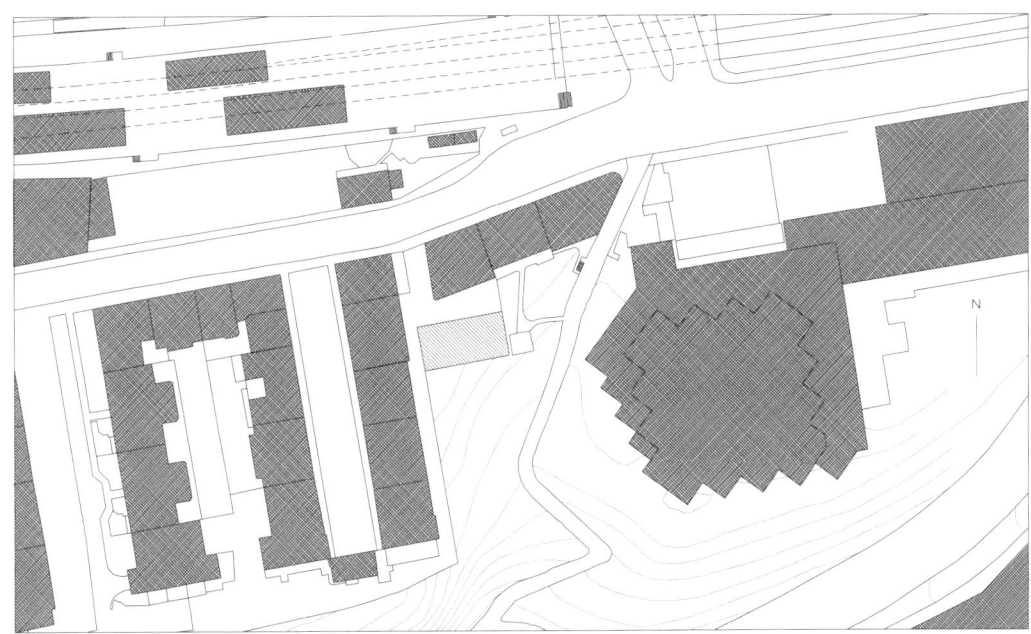

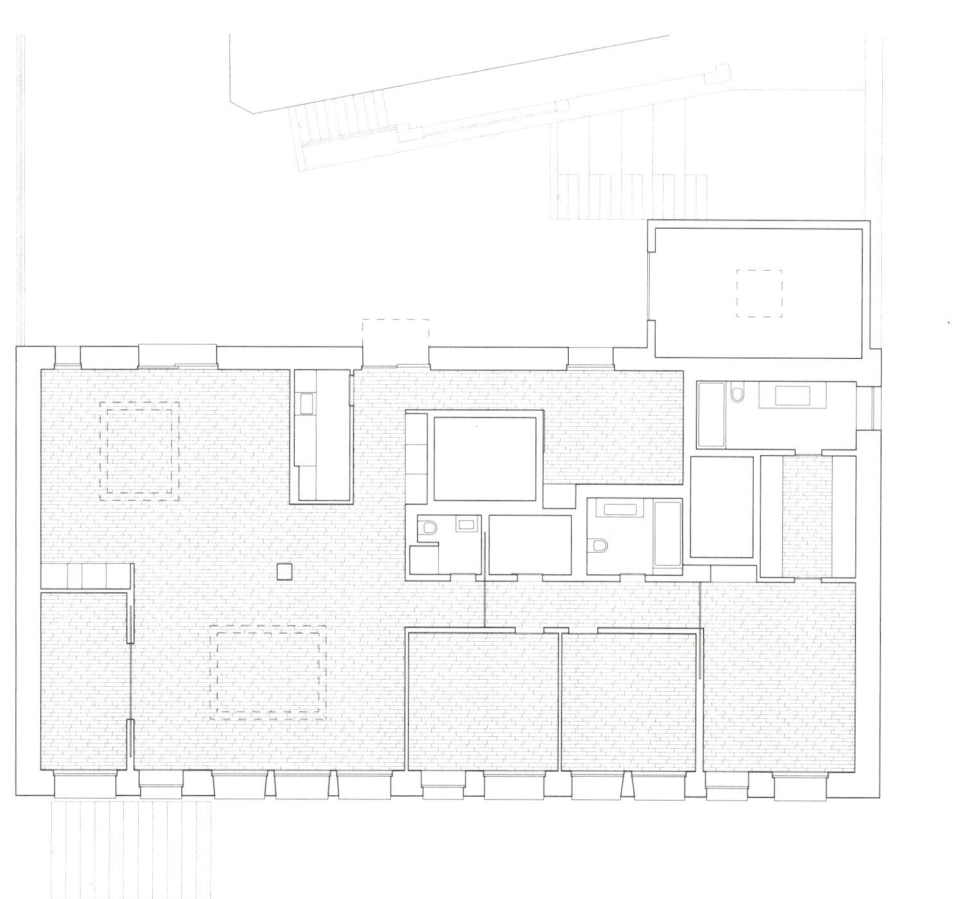

Zwei Villen in Chambésy, Genf / Two villas in Chambésy, Geneva

Das Projekt für zwei Doppelhäuser in Chambésy – in einem schon seit langer Zeit bestehenden Wohnviertel am Genfer Stadtrand – geht in vielfältiger Art auf den unmittelbaren Kontext ein. Die beiden Häuser fügen sich in den morphologischen Massstab der grossen Nachbarbauten ein und sind zur Strasse hin so organisert, dass sie den Eindruck eines zusammenhängenden Ensembles vermitteln. Auf der Rückseite ist die Tatsache, dass es sich um zwei Gebäude handelt, hingegen deutlich ablesbar. Hier wird der Massstab gebrochen. Stark vorspringende Vordächer definieren einen Aussenraum für jede Wohneinheit, der Privatsphäre ermöglicht, während gleichzeitig die durchgehenden, offenen Gartenanlagen erhalten bleiben.

Innen findet sich an der Treppe im Zentrum des Grundrisses ein Raum von doppelter Geschosshöhe, der eine Verbindung zwischen allen Innenräumen schafft. Dieser Raum ermöglicht einerseits eine natürliche Belichtung des Wohnungsinneren und setzt andererseits einen vertikalen Akzent gegenüber der ansonsten vorherrschend horizontalen Blickführung.

Set within a well established residential area in the outskirts of Geneva, the project for two semi-detached houses in Chambésy offers a diversified response to its immediate context. Inscribed within the morphological scale of the large neighbouring houses, the two houses are grouped on the street frontage, giving the impression of forming a single unit. To the rear, the building is clearly articulated into two separate units, contradicting the scale initially perceived on the street. Large cantilevered roofs articulate two exterior balcony spaces, providing intimacy to each whilst preserving the continuous space of the garden.

Internally, a double-height space accompanies the stair at the heart of the plan, connecting all the internal spaces. This opening enables light to enter deep into the building with a strong vertical emphasis in an otherwise dominantly horizontal composition.

Jaccaud Spicher Architectes
Bauzeit/Construction: 2013–2015
Bauherr/Client: privat/private
Team: Jean-Paul Jaccaud, Lionel Spicher, Luca Berolini, Diane Gämperle
Fachplaner/Consultants: B. Devaud SA

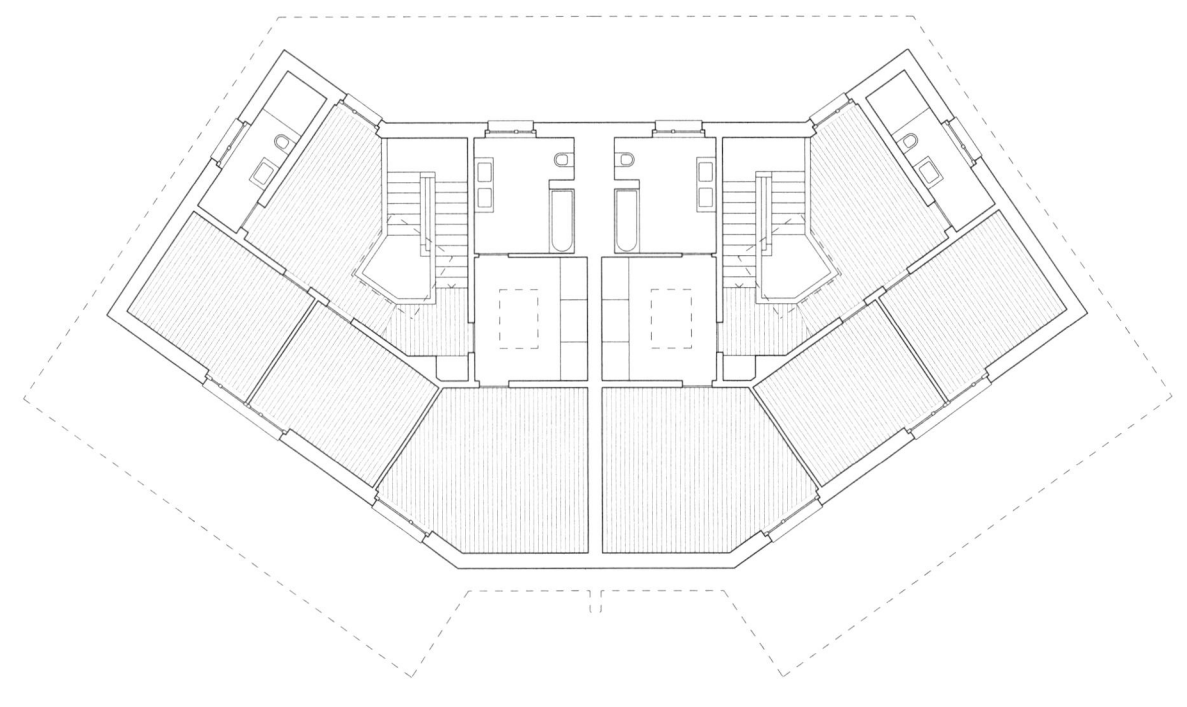

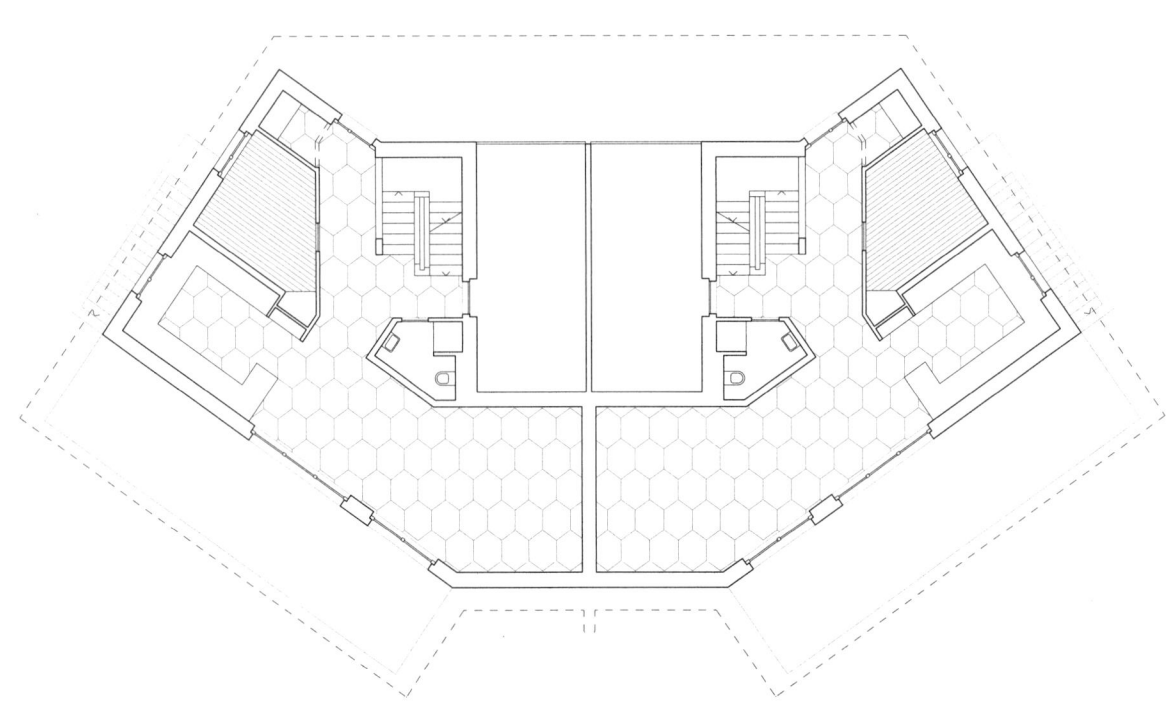

52

Chalet in La Forclaz, Evolène

Das Chalet mit zwei Wohnungen in La Forclaz im Val d'Herens ist eine zeitgemässe Neuinterpretation einer historischen Gebäudetypologie, die in dieser Region sehr präsent ist. Da die Grundstücke in den Dorfkernen relativ klein sind, wurden die Chalets hier in die Höhe entwickelt und erreichen vier oder fünf Geschosse.

Das Projekt befindet sich an der Schnittstelle zwischen dem historischen Gefüge des «alten» Dorfs La Forclaz und neueren Chalets, die in den 1970er und 1980er Jahren erbaut wurden. Mit seiner deutlich hervortretenden Volumetrie, die jene der Gebäude des historischen Dorfs fortsetzt, verbindet das Projekt diese beiden unterschiedlichen Bereiche.

Im Inneren verteilen sich die beiden Wohnungen über jeweils zwei Etagen mit einem sehr komplizierten Zuschnitt, der es erlaubt, die Geschosshöhen zu variieren. In den Wohnzimmern, die durch nach Süden ausgerichtete Balkone verlängert wurden, öffnen sich grosse Glasfenster zur Landschaft.

Chalet in La Forclaz, Evolene

The project for a chalet with two dwellings at the Forclaz in the Val d'Hérens proposes a contemporary interpretation of a historical type very present in the region of 4 to 5-storey high timber chalets. Located at the junction between the "old" village of the Forclaz and more recent constructions from the 1970s and 1980s the projects attempt to stitch these two fabrics together by its prominent volume that prolongs those of the neighbouring historical centre.

Internally, two dwellings are articulated each over two floors with an interlocking section that allows for differentiated ceiling heights in each space. Large openings frame the surrounding mountain landscape from the living areas which are prolonged by south-facing balconies.

Jaccaud Zein Architects
Bauzeit/Construction: 2012–2015
Bauherr/Client: privat/private
Team: Jean-Paul Jaccaud, Tanya Zein Jaccaud, Diogo Fonseca Lopes, Gaëtan Evéquoz
Fachplaner/Consultants: Charpente Concept, Sorane SA

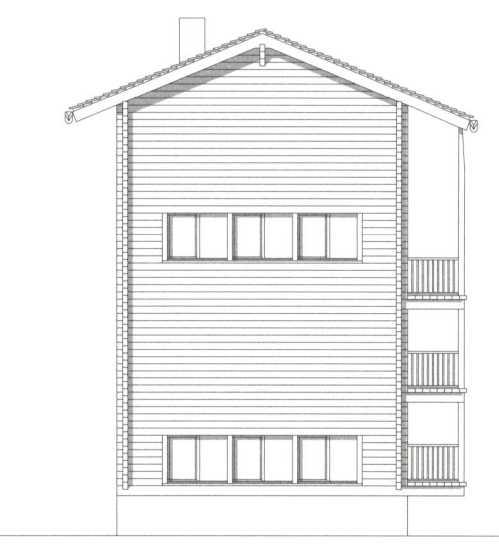

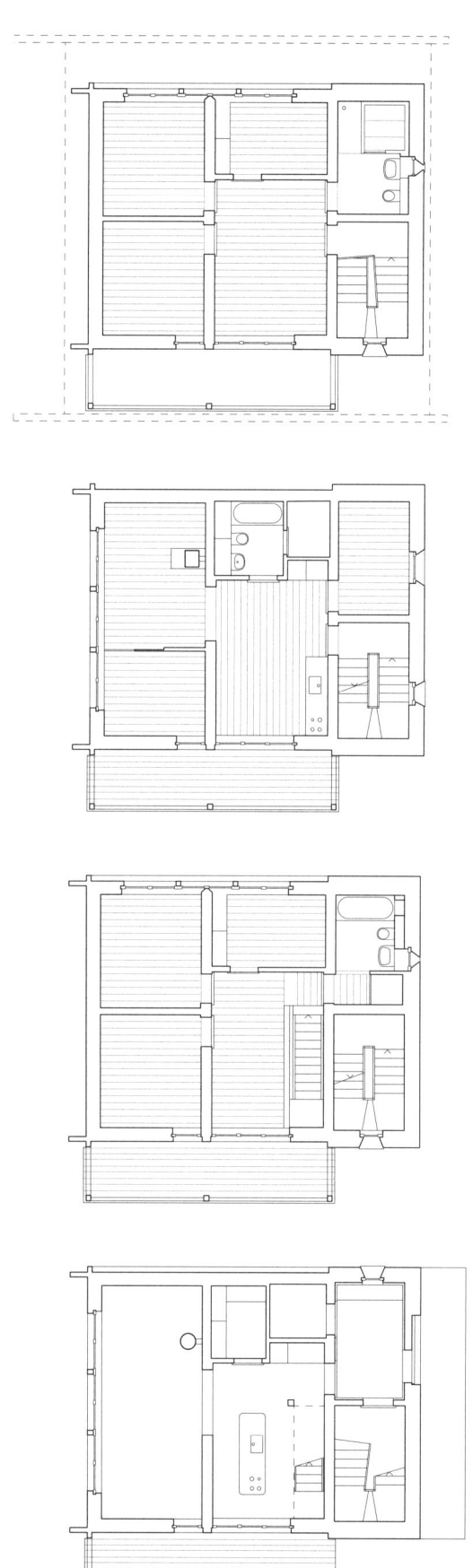

Fassaden- und Wohnungssanierung, Le Lignon, Genf

Façade and apartment renovation, Le Lignon, Geneva

Die zwischen 1963 und 1971 errichtete Cité du Lignon ist mit 2370 Wohnungen, die sich auf ein über 1 Kilometer langes Gebäude mit bis zu 18 Geschossen und zwei Turmbauten am Ufer der Rhône verteilen, der grösste Wohnkomplex der Schweiz. Die Gebäude sind seit 2001 als Denkmal eingestuft. Die Fassaden mussten allerdings dringend saniert werden, um sie an die heute geltenden Energiestandards anzupassen. Im Jahr 2010 wurde vom TSAM-Labor der ETH Lausanne eine detaillierte Untersuchung angestellt, um eine Strategie für die Sanierung der Fassaden und Gemeinschaftsflächen zu erarbeiten.

Jaccaud Spicher Architectes wurden beauftragt, die TSAM-Untersuchung umzusetzen. Im ersten Schritt sollte die Fallstudie auf die Gesamtheit aller speziellen Bedingungen angewendet werden. Im nächsten Schritt galt es, die Baugenehmigung von den zuständigen Behörden zu erwirken und schliesslich die Renovierungsmassnahmen bezüglich der Fassaden, Flure und Gemeinschaftsflächen mit den verschiedenen Eigentümern durchzuführen.

Gleichzeitig zu den Arbeiten an der Gebäudehülle wurden auch einige Wohnungen renoviert, um Modelle zu schaffen, die im grossen Massstab wiederholt werden können. Bei diesen Renovierungen wurde im Wesentlichen eine Palette von Materialien und Details festgelegt, die dem originalen Charakter der Gebäude entsprechen.

Built between 1963 and 1971, the Cité du Lignon is the largest housing complex in Switzerland with 2,730 apartments distributed between a linear "bar" building over a kilometre long and two tower blocks facing on to the River Rhône.

The buildings have a strong heritage value and were subsequently listed in 2001. The façades however require renovation and adaptation to meet contemporary energy standards and ensure their long-term stabilisation. A detailed study was carried out to this effect in 2010 by the TSAM laboratory at EPFL that determined a strategy for the renovation of the façades and common areas.

Jaccaud Spicher Architects were commissioned to implement the TSAM study, obtaining planning permission and carrying out renovation work with various owners for the façades, common areas, walkways and entrance areas.

In parallel with the work on the envelope, renovation work was carried out on the interiors of a number of apartments, creating model units to be replicated by establishing a palette of materials and details in keeping with the original character of the building.

Jaccaud Spicher Architectes
Bauzeit/Construction: 2012–2015
Bauherr/Client: privat/private
Team: Jean-Paul Jaccaud, Lionel Spicher, Fanny Noël, Benoît Cousin, Stephan Gratzer, Marco Ferrari

Erste Sanierungsetappe, Fassadenrenovation, Avenue du Lignon 49

First stage of rehabilitation, renovated façade, No 49 Avenue du Lignon

No 49 Avenue du Lignon

1 Rahmen aus Fichtenholz, aufgebracht auf die beibehaltene bestehende Zarge. Er verschwindet in der Dicke der Profile und ist von aussen nicht sichtbar
2 Die erhaltenen Öffnungen mit einer Aussenverkleidung aus Aluminium und einer Innenverkleidung aus Kiefernholz. Überrahmen aus Fichtenholz, angesetzt an die bestehenden Öffnungen
3 Ursprüngliche einfache Innenverglasung, ersetzt durch eine neue Isolierverglasung 4/20/4 (mm) (Aussenverkleidung aus vorgespanntem Isolierglas)
4 Neue Lamellenjalousie, eingebracht in den Fensterkasten aus Aluminiumbändern. Festes Material, Ursprungsfarbe Weiss. Breite 25 mm
5 Belüftungsöffnungen, schräg in den bestehenden Holzrahmen gebohrt
6 Manuelle Steuerung der Jalousie durch aussen angebrachte Stangen gemäss dem Ursprungsmodell
7 Griff mit einem oberen Überstand von 70 mm
8 Neue Isolierung aus Glaswolle, 30+60 mm, l=0,032 W/mK
9 Dampfsperre
10 Gipsplatte, 20 mm, l=0,40 W/mK
11 Fensterbrett aus Holz
12 Bestehende Heizkörper, vorab um ca. 10 cm versetzt
13 Luftzwischenraum

1 Spruce frame, attached to the retained existing case. It disappears in the thickness of the profiles and is invisible from the outside.
2 Retained openings with an exterior aluminium envelope and pine interior cladding. Spruce top frame, placed at existing openings
3 Original single glazing, replaced by new insulating glass 4/20/4 (mm) (exterior envelope of tempered insulating glass)
4 New Venetian blind, inserted into the aluminium-band window case. Solid material, original colour white. Breadth 25 mm
5 Ventilation apertures, drilled diagonally into the existing wooden frame
6 Manual adjustment of the blind using outer attachment of a bar, in accordance with the original model
7 Grip with an upper protrusion of 70 mm
8 New glass wool insulation, 30+60 mm, l=0.032 W/mK
9 Vapour barrier
10 Plasterboard, 20 mm, l=0.40 W/mK
11 Wooden windowsill
12 Existing radiators, previously shifted by approx. 10 cm
13 Air gap

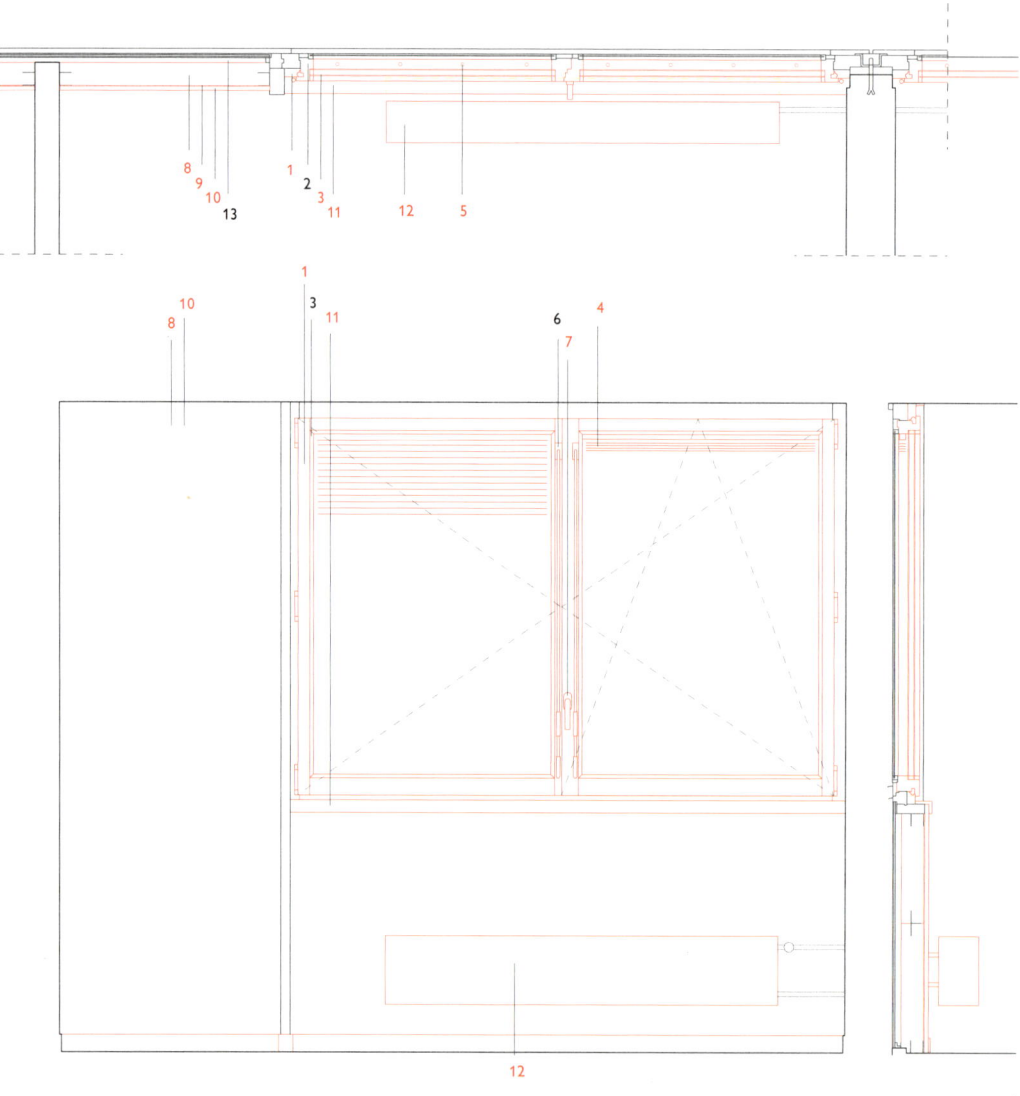

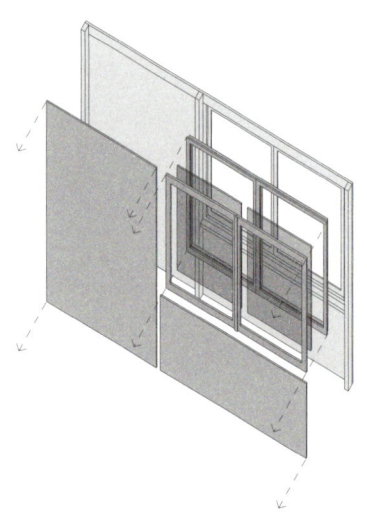

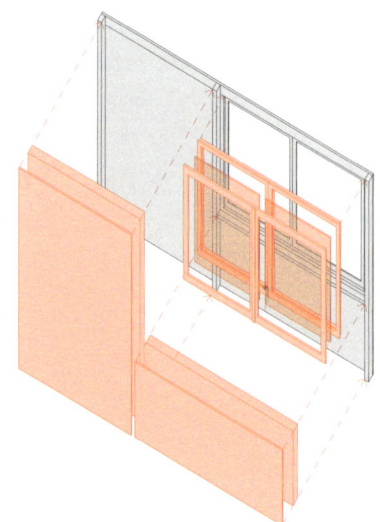

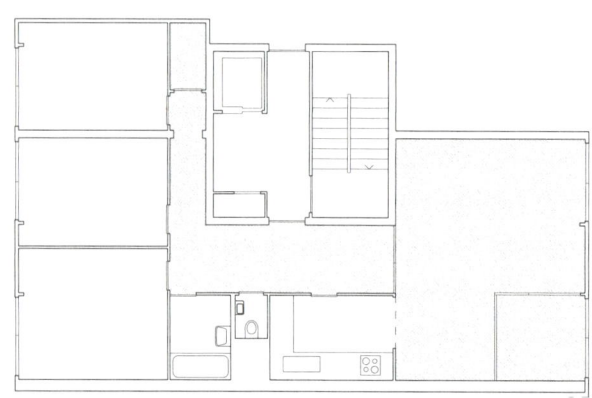

74

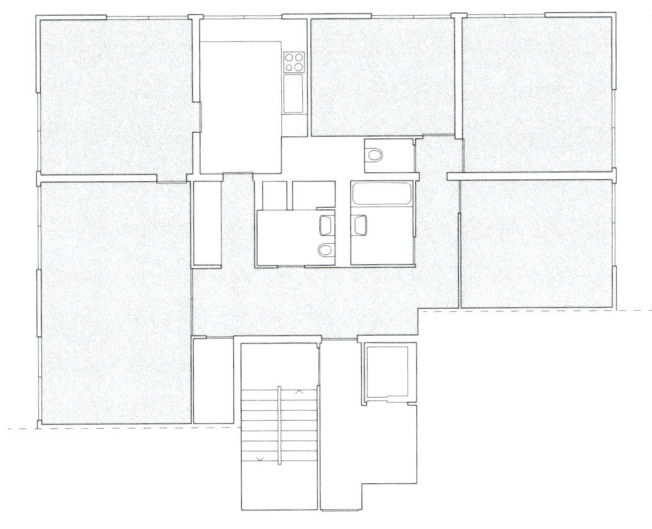

Renovation eines Gebäudes an der Albert Street, London

Building renovation in Albert Street, London

Im Zuge der Renovierung und Erweiterung eines Reihenhauses von 1840 in der Albert Street im Londoner Bezirk Camden bot sich die Gelegenheit, die Feinheiten der räumlichen und typologischen Konfigurationen der frühviktorianischen Wohnarchitektur zu analysieren und zu verstehen. Das Verständnis der Hierarchien, Proportionen und Verteilungsmuster des Hauses floss später in das Projekt am Shepherdess Walk ein. Das Projekt in der Albert Street bot darüber hinaus die Möglichkeit, eine Materialpalette von Rauputz über Holz bis zu Materialien, die der Patinierung unterliegen, zu testen, die mittlerweile bei mehreren anderen Projekten eingesetzt wurde.

Das Haus war ursprünglich ein Stockwerk niedriger als die anschliessenden Gebäude. Um die Strassenfront zu vereinheitlichen, wurde ein fünftes Geschoss aufgestockt, das sich dem Profil der benachbarten Dächer anpasst. Innen wurden neue Treppen eingefügt, um die neue Etage zu erschliessen. Sie verlängern die elegante Gestalt der originalen «halb aufgesattelten amerikanischen» Treppe.

The project for the renovation and extension of an 1840 terraced house on Albert Street in Camden Town was an opportunity to analyse and understand the subtleties of the spatial and typological configurations of early Victorian domestic architecture. The understanding of the hierarchies, proportions and distributive patterns of the house found a strong echo in the later Shepherdess Walk Project. It was also an opportunity to test a material palette of rough plaster, timber and materials subject to patination in situ which has been used in several other projects since then.

The house was originally built over four floors and a fifth floor was added with a renewed profile of the roof. Originally the house had been built one story lower than its neighbours and this extension reinstated a continuity of frontage to the streetscape. Internally, new stairs were added to reach the top floor, continuing the elegant existing figure of the "american semi hung" Victorian stairs.

Jaccaud Zein Architects
Bauzeit/Construction: 2011–2012
Bauherr/Client: privat/private
Team: Jean-Paul Jaccaud, Tanya Zein, Fanny Noël, Valentin Bussard

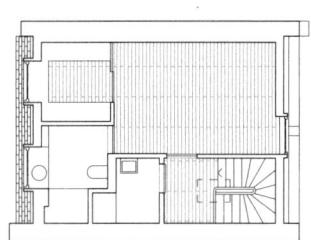

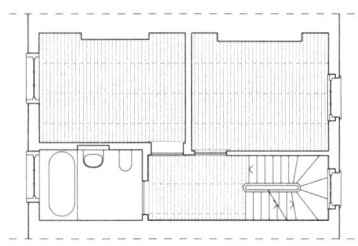

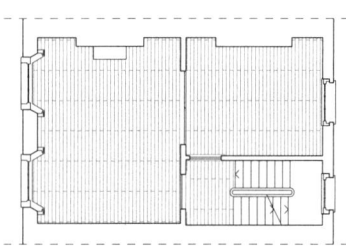

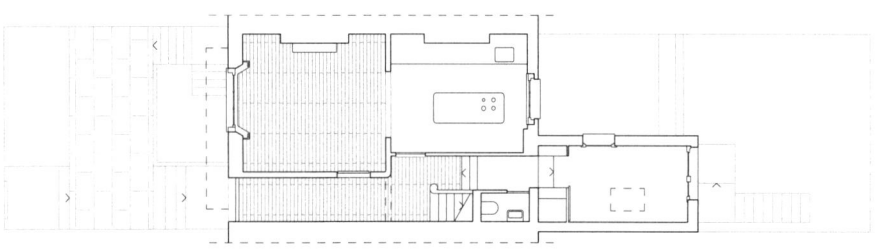

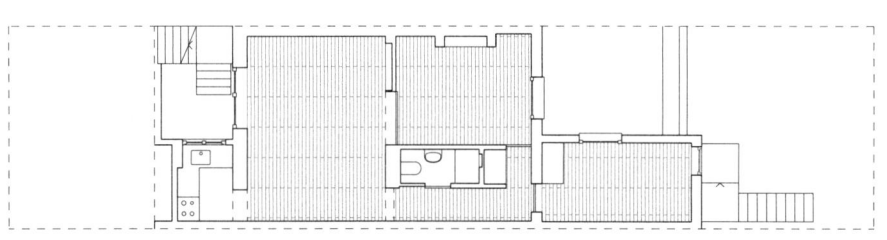

5 m

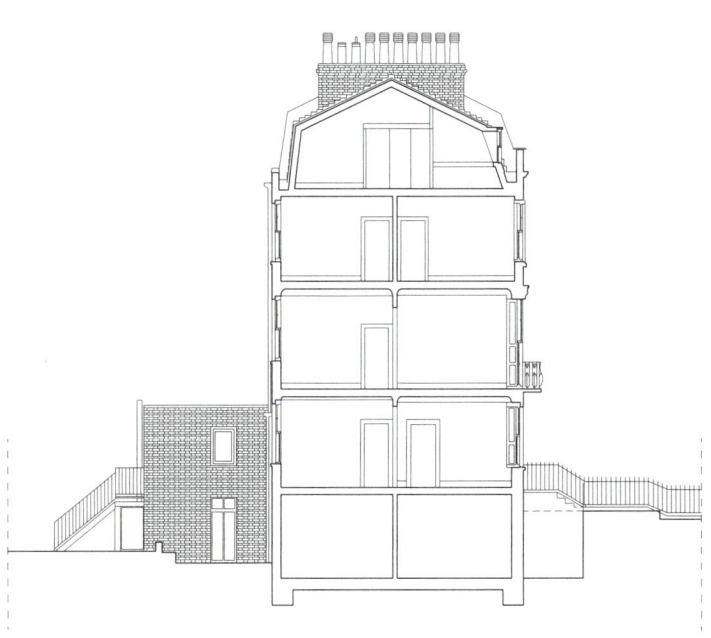

5 m

Wohnanlage, Shepherdess Walk, London

Housing in Shepherdess Walk, London

Das an der Kreuzung Shepherdess Walk und Wenlock Street gelegene Wohngebäude vermittelt zwischen den verschiedenen historischen Spuren und formalen Eigenschaften des Geländes. Die drei Reihenhäuser und das Apartmentgebäude sind stark in ihrem Kontext verankert. Die Gebäudemasse vergrössert sich vom Einfamilienwohnhausmassstab am Shepherdess Walk zu dem höheren Apartmentgebäude, mit dem das Projekt an die sozialen Wohnbauten der Nachkriegszeit an der Wenlock Street anschliesst.

Für die Reihenhäuser und die Apartments wurde eine Aufgliederung in Zwischengeschosse entwickelt. Diese Konfiguration erlaubt die Gruppierung der Zimmer rund um Räume von doppelter Höhe, sodass sich eine grosszügige räumliche Kontinuität ergibt.

Die Gliederung in Halbgeschosse ermöglicht zudem eine grosse Nutzungsflexibilität bei den Apartments; jede Einheit kann so aufgeteilt werden, dass jede der aufgeteilten Wohnungen einen eigenen Zugang zum Treppenhaus hat. Damit ist die Möglichkeit gegeben, die Grösse anzupassen und eine Adaption an sich ändernde Bedürfnisse vorzunehmen, wenn etwa die Kinder heranwachsen, das frühere Büro als Wohnung genutzt, ein Teil der Wohnung vermietet oder einzelne Zimmer auf andere Weise als bisher genutzt werden sollen.

Situated at the corner of Shepherdess Walk and Wenlock Street, the project mediates between the different historical conditions and formal qualities of the site to propose a terrace of houses and an apartment building with a strong sense of place. The massing of the buildings increases in height from the domestic scale of the houses on Shepherdess Walk to the taller apartment building that stitches the development into the context of post-war housing blocks that extend beyond on Wenlock Street.

A split-level section was developed that was applied to both houses and apartments. This configuration allows for the juxtaposition of rooms with different usages around double-height connected spaces, offering a sense of spatial generosity and continuity.

The split-level arrangement introduced a strong potential for flexibility for the apartments, allowing for possible subdivisions within each unit with multiple access to the stairwell. This flexibility allows for a possible fragmentation of scale and an evolution of use through time to meet the demands of multiple occupancy, of children growing up, of partial rental of the unit, of working from home or just varying use of the different rooms.

Jaccaud Zein Architects
Bauzeit/Construction: 2012–2016
Bauherr/Client: Solidspace
Team: Jean-Paul Jaccaud, Tanya Zein, Fanny Noël, Diogo Fonseca Lopes, Stephan Gratzer
Fachplaner/Consultants: Conisbee, Measur, AZ Urban Studio

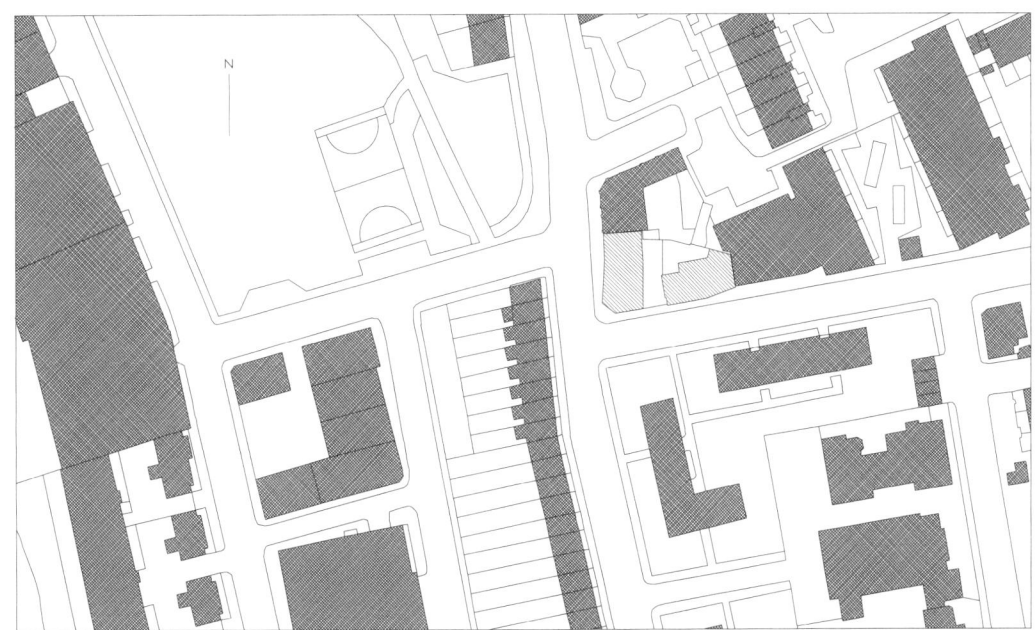

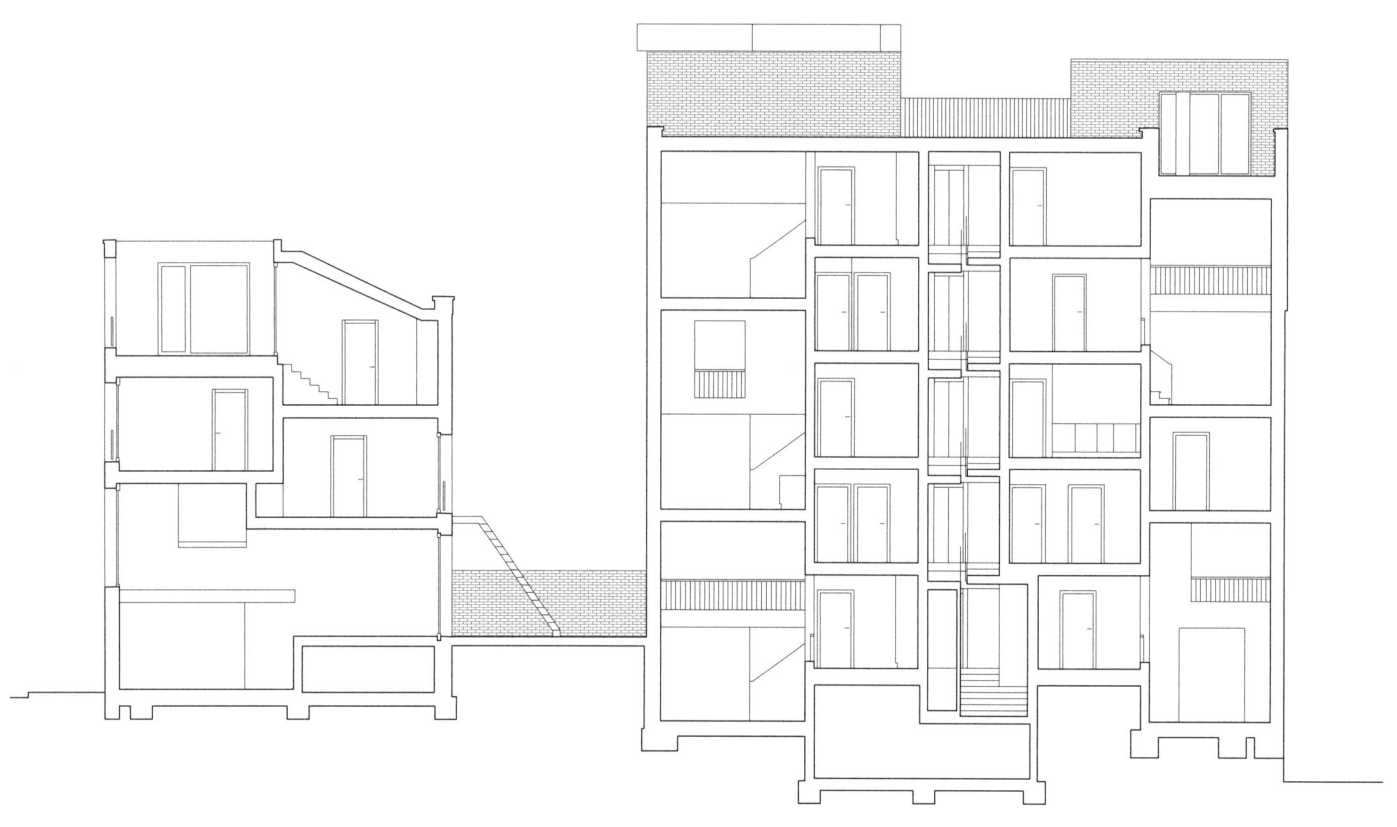

Wohnanlage, Sentier des Saules, Genf

Sentier des Saules housing block, Geneva

Das Leitprinzip der neuen genossenschaftlichen Wohnanlage bildet die Erinnerung: Die Identität des Projektes wurde intuitiv in der Kontinuität der industriellen Vergangenheit des Geländes verankert. Auch wenn Nutzungsänderungen die Wahrnehmung der alten Werksgebäude verändert haben, bestimmt ihre Präsenz dennoch stark das Ufer der Rhône in Genf. Das Projekt fügt sich mit seiner Masse und seinem architektonischen Ausdruck deshalb in eine grössere Figur ein, die eine Verbindung zu den beiden Gebäuden aufnimmt, die das Gelände flankieren. Drei starke Formen treten somit in Erscheinung und bilden im Zusammenklang eine präzise und sich klar abzeichnende Gestalt, die die Identität des Viertels stärkt und heraushebt.

Das Projekt schlägt verschiedene Wohnungstypen innerhalb eines Gebäudes vor: genossenschaftliche Familienwohnungen, Wohnungen für Studenten sowie Mehrgenerationenwohnungen vom Cluster-Typ. Diese verschiedenen Typen wurden unter ständiger Rücksicht auf «Schwellen» und Orte des geselligen Austauschs miteinander verbunden, um das Gemeinschaftsgefühl der Bewohner zu stärken. So erweitern sich oberhalb des gemeinsamen Erdgeschosses die Erschliessungsflächen vor den Fahrstühlen und Treppenabsätzen zu einem grossen Balkon, den sich drei oder vier Wohnungen teilen. Jede Wohnung öffnet sich zu diesem Balkon mit einem Mehrzweckraum, der als Küche, Esszimmer, Eingangshalle, Arbeitsraum oder Treffpunkt dienen kann. Eine tiefe Schwelle trennt diese Räume von den Balkonen und lässt den Bewohnern die Wahl, wie viel Offenheit oder Privatsphäre sie wünschen.

The identity of this cooperative housing project is strongly informed by historical memory in an attempt to preserve continuity with the industrial past of the area. If programmatic changes have renewed the reading of the surrounding industrial buildings, their presence still strongly qualifies the banks of the River Rhône in Geneva. The project inscribes itself by its massing and its architectural expression in a wider figure linked to the two buildings which flank it on the riverbank. Three strong forms appear, creating a precise large-scale entity reinforcing the identity of the site.

The project proposes different types of housing within a single volume, with cooperative family-orientated housing, student housing and multigenerational shared "cluster" type accommodation. This juxtaposition of types is done with a constant preoccupation with thresholds and places for sociability that will help convey a strong sense of community to the inhabitants. Above the ground floor, the circulation widens in front of the lifts to offer a large balcony shared by three of four flats. Each dwelling opens onto the balcony by a "common room" which serves simultaneously as a dining room, entrance hall, kitchen and workspace. A deep threshold separates these rooms from the balconies, leaving to the occupants the choice of the level of openness that they require.

Jaccaud Spicher Architectes
Wettbewerb/Competition: 2014,
1. Preis / 1st prize
Bauherr/Client:
Coopératives Codha et Cigüe
Team: Jean-Paul Jaccaud, Lionel Spicher, Bastien Guy, Inês Morão Dias, Nicolas Schmutz
Fachplaner/Consultants: Ott et Uldry, MAB ingénierie SA, Putalaz SA, Pierre Buclin SA, AcouConsult Sàrl

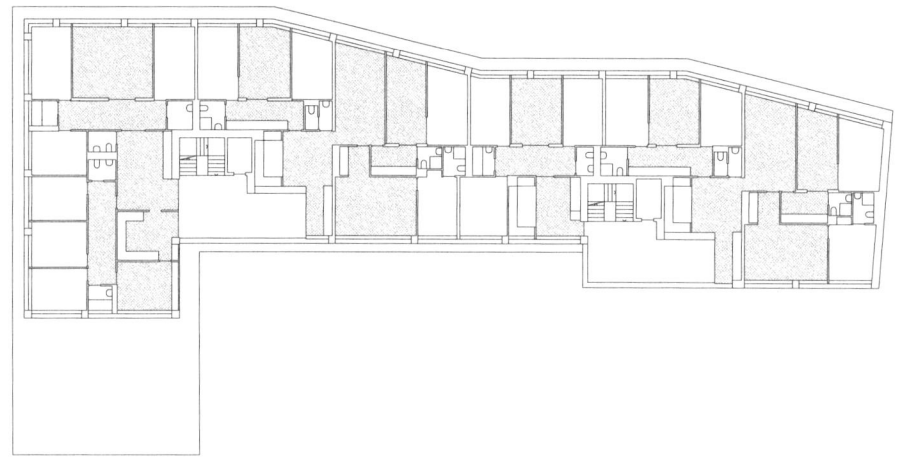
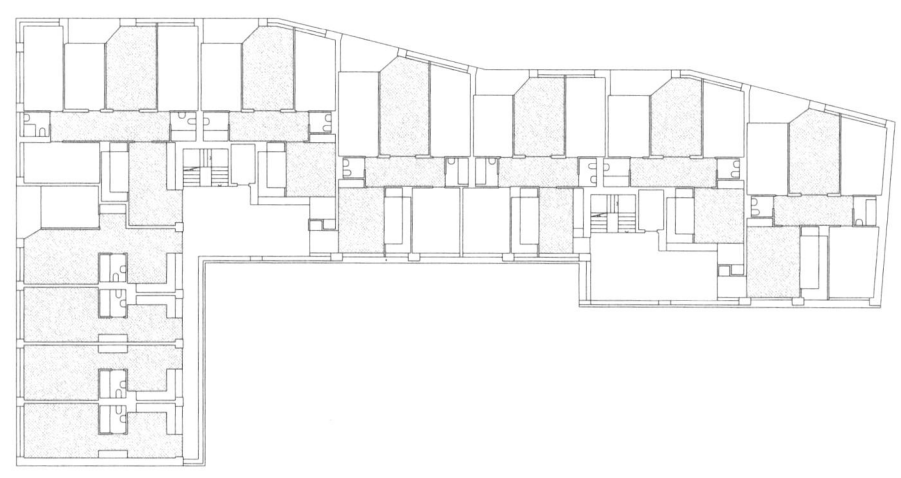
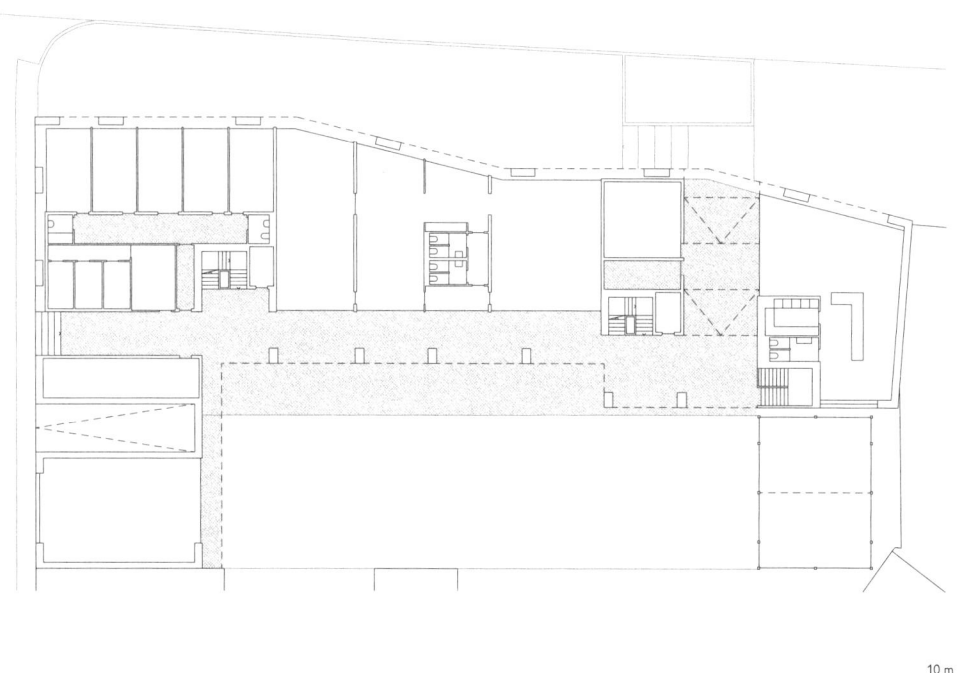

10 m

Wohnanlage, Eaux-Vives, Genf

Housing block in Eaux-Vives, Geneva

Trotz des kleinen Massstabs liegt das Grundstück an der Kreuzung der Rue des Cordiers und der Rue des Vollandes im Zentrum einer komplexen städtebaulichen Situation. Das gegenwärtig vorhandene Gebäude rückt leicht in die Strasse vor und bekräftigt damit seine Präsenz in deren Verlängerung. In seiner Materialität und seinem Charakter schliesst es an die Gebäude der Hausnummern 58–70 der Rue des Vollandes an, die ein ausdrucksstarkes Ensemble bilden.

Das Projekt will diese subtil bekräftigte Präsenz des Gebäudeensembles in der Rue des Vollandes erhalten, indem es das Vorrücken des Gebäudes in die Rue des Cordiers beibehält. Durch seine eingefaltete Volumetrie fungiert das neue Gebäude zugleich als bestätigender Abschluss des Ensembles in der Rue des Vollandes und als Anschluss an die Gebäude in der Rue des Cordiers. Die Ecke erhält eine leicht abgeschrägte Form, um den grossen Massstab der Öffnung zum See aufzugreifen und den Wohnblock leicht auf diesen auszurichten.

Während die Grundrissform des Gebäudes subtil seine «Differenz» betont, streben sein Ausdruck, seine Masse, der regelmässige Rhythmus der Fenster und seine Materialität nach einer Vermittlung zu den Fassaden der Nachbargebäude und rufen das gegenwärtig vorhandene Gebäude ins Gedächtnis.

In spite of its Small scale, the site at the corner of the Rue des Cordiers and the Rue des Vollandes is at the heart of a complex urban situation. The building currently existing on the site advances slightly, signifying a distinct presence in the otherwise linear alignment of the street. The existing building completes a series of continuous developments on the Rue des Vollandes that give the street a distinct character.

The project proposes to keep the subtly suggested advance of the existing building on the Rue des Cordiers. By its folded volume, the building acts as a "figurehead" for the Rue des Vollandes buildings whilst at the same time stitching the building back into the Rue des Cordiers. The angle is given a slightly slanted geometry to address the large scale of the opening of the site onto the lake and subtly give the urban block an orientation onto it. This angle is completed by a double-height loggia at the top of the building, which reinforces the shift in scale with the opening on the lake.

If the plan shape of the building subtly suggests "difference", the expression of the building, its scale and the regular rhythms of its façades attempt a mediation between the neighbouring buildings and a memory of the existing one. This continuity is also perceptible by the presence of the prefabricated concrete plinth that prolongs the ones of the neighbouring buildings. This allows the complexity of the form to appear only at second glance as a subtle background sign.

Jaccaud Spicher Architectes
Wettbewerb/Competition: 2012, 1. Preis / 1st prize
Bauherr/Client: Ville de Genève
Team: Jean-Paul Jaccaud, Lionel Spicher, Stephan Gratzer, Ines Morão Dias, Hildur Yr Ottosdottir, Anna Salvioni, Diogo Fonseca Lopes, Henriette Ritschel, Luke Lagier, Gaëtan Evequoz
Fachplaner/Consultants: EDMS SA, Pierre Buclin SA, R. Moser SA, Rigot Rieben SA

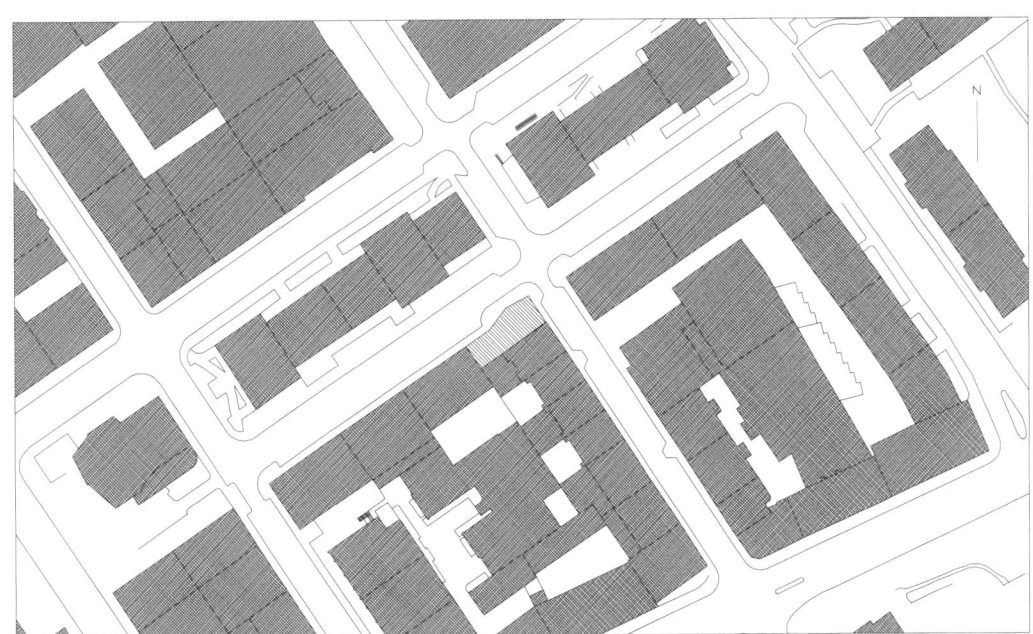

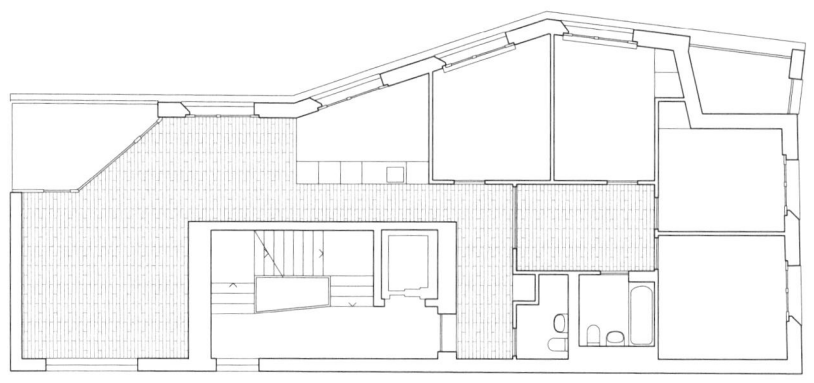

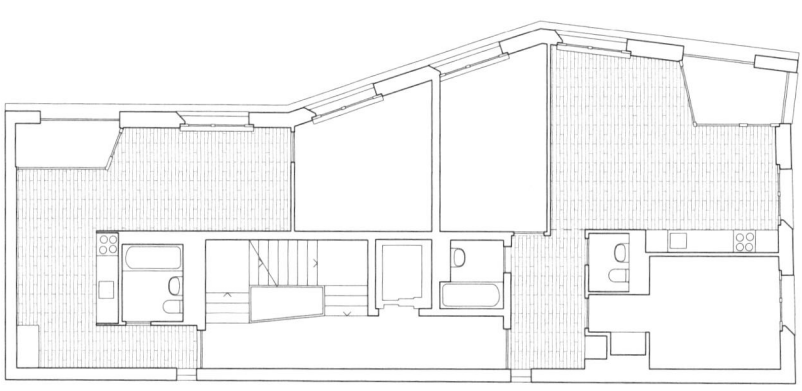

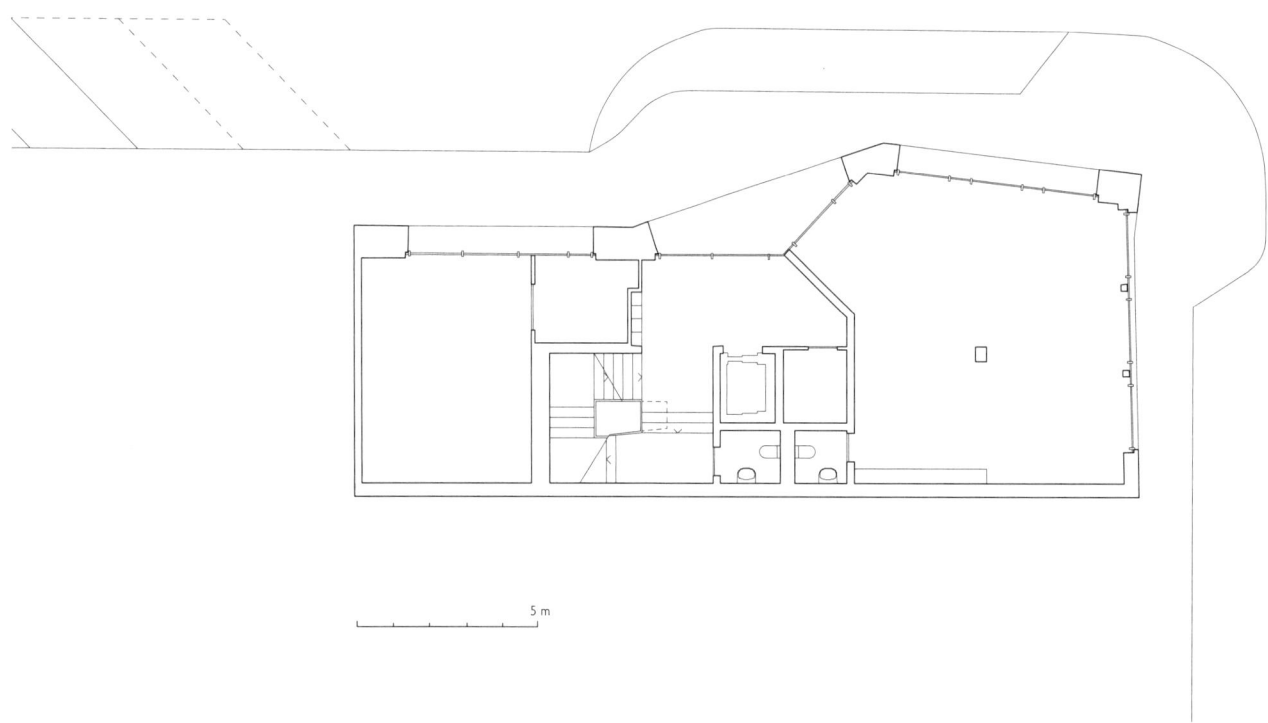

5 m

Wohnanlage, Communaux d'Ambilly, Genf

Housing block at the Communaux d'Ambilly, Geneva

Die Anlage basiert auf einem Masterplan von Atelier Bonnet und vereint Sozialwohnungen in einem einzigen, stark gegliederten Gebäudevolumen.

Das Prinzip der Eckigkeit liegt der räumlichen Konfiguration der Wohnungen zugrunde, und wir haben versucht, die Zahl der Ecksituationen an den Fassaden entsprechend zu maximieren. Das Prinzip verweist auf historische Beispiele, unter anderem auf die Gebäude Hans Scharouns in der Berliner Siemensstadt und auf die Bauten von Marc Saugey in Miremenot le Crêt. Die Wohnungen haben alle eine doppelte Ausrichtung; in fast allen Fällen gliedern sie sich um einen «zentralen» Eckbalkon. Diese Konfiguration ermöglicht es, die schöne Aussicht, die das Gelände bietet, optimal zu nutzen und so die Landschaft in die Privatsphäre der einzelnen Wohnungen hineinzubringen.

Um jedem Aufgang eine deutliche Identität zu geben und wichtige Zonen des geselligen Austauschs und der Begegnung herauszuheben, beruht das Prinzip der Verteilung auf dem des Innenhofs. Die Wohnungen verteilen sich um grosszügige, von oben belichtete Räume. Vorgefertigter Beton ist das bevorzugte Fassadenmaterial. Alle Wohnungen erhalten Fensterrahmen aus Holz. Diese Materialkombination verweist auf historische Vorbilder der ländlichen Architektur des Genfer Umlands und greift auf zeitgenössische Art ihren Ausdruck, ihre Farbigkeit und ihre Materialität auf.

The project is based on a masterplan established by the Atelier Bonnet and integrates social housing within a strongly articulated volume.

The principle of angularity is at the heart of the spatial configuration of the dwellings and we have attempted to maximise the extent of angle situations on the façades. This principle refers to historical precedents, amongst many the Siemenstadt buildings by Hans Scharoun in Berlin or Marc Saugey's Miremont le Crêt housing in Geneva. The apartments all have a double orientation, organised in almost all cases around a "central" corner balcony. This configuration allows them to benefit from the beautiful views that the site offers and to interiorise the landscape into the intimacy of the dwellings.

In order to give each part of the building a distinct character, the distributive principle is based on inner courtyards with apartments grouped around generous top-lit open spaces. Prefabricated concrete appeared as the principal material for the façades, in conjunction with timber frame windows. This material combination establishes links with historic precedents of rural architecture in the Geneva countryside, with a contemporary echo of their expression, their tonal qualities and their materiality.

Jaccaud Spicher Architectes
Concours/Competition: 2014, Preisträger/lauréat
Bauherr/Client: Batima/C2i
Team: Jean-Paul Jaccaud, Lionel Spicher, Stephan Gratzer, Ines Morão Dias, Luke Lagier
Fachplaner/Consultants: ESM ingénierie SA, Weimann SA, Eggtelsa SA, AcouConsult Sàrl

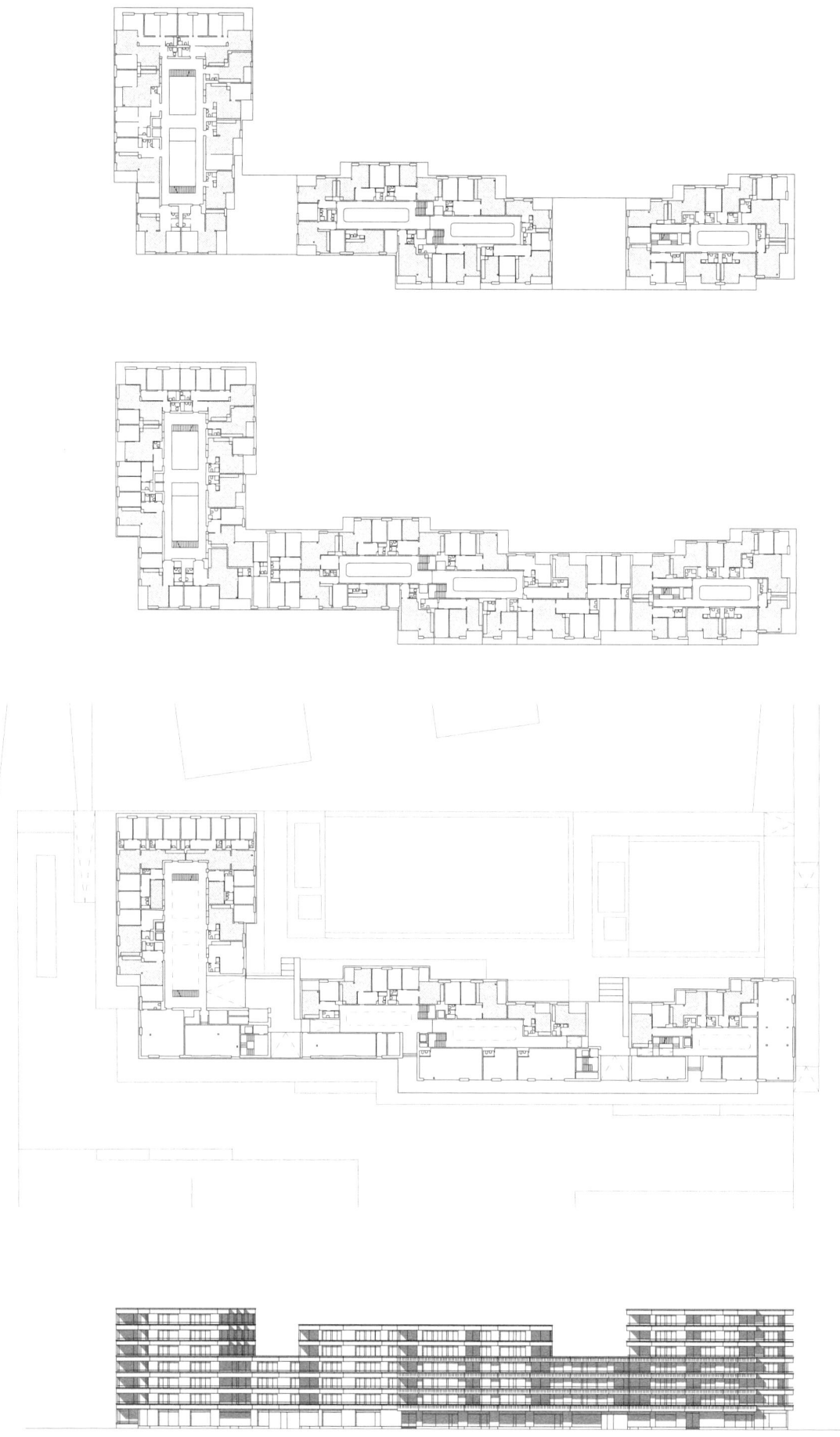

Wohnanlage, Les Grottes, Genf

Housing block in Les Grottes, Geneva

Das Projekt sieht eine auffällige Form vor, deren präzise gegliederte Volumetrie in verschiedener Weise auf das unmittelbare Umfeld eingeht. Der Grundriss hat eine radiale Gestalt, der die wichtigsten Ausrichtungen rund um das Grundstück hervorhebt: auf den angrenzenden Parc des Cropettes, auf die Rue des Grottes und auf den öffentlichen Raum neben der Rue Louis Favre. Die Wohnungen sind so unterteilt, dass sie optimal von der Gebäudeausrichtung nach Süden und auf das Viertel in der Rue des Grottes profitieren. Das ermöglicht eine ideale Orientierung in Bezug auf die natürliche Belichtung und bietet gleichzeitig von den Wohnungen aus weite Ausblicke die Strassen hinunter.

Die Wohnungen sind im Inneren in eine offene Raumfolge gegliedert, die auf ein grosses, nach drei Seiten ausgerichtetes Wohnzimmer an den Ecken des Gebäudes zuführt. Diese Aufteilung ist mit einem Foyer verankert, das gross genug ist, um für Wohnzwecke genutzt zu werden, und den zentralen Raum des Innenbereichs bildet. Die Schlafzimmer gehen von diesem Flur ab, eines davon als dessen direkte räumliche Verlängerung hinter einer Schiebetür. Diese Konfiguration ermöglicht eine flexible Nutzung und sorgt gleichzeitig für eine grosszügige natürliche Belichtung in der Mitte des Wohnungsgrundrisses.

The project proposes a strong form, volumetrically articulated to offer varying responses to its immediate context. The project mediates between the large scale of the park and the buildings set within it, and the closed urban blocks of the Grottes area. The plan organises a radial figure which gives significance to the principal orientations of the site, the adjacent Parc des Cropettes, the Rue des Grottes and the public space adjacent to the Rue Louis Favre.

This form provides ideal sun orientation and distant views along the streets from the apartments within. It also generates a small urban square that follows the succession of spaces linking the station to the South to the housing complexes north of the Rue Louis Favre.

Typologically, the apartments are organised with triple orientations on the angles, with large entrance halls establishing a generous threshold with the stairwell beyond.

Jaccaud Spicher Architectes
Wettbewerb/Competition: 2010,
1. Preis / 1st prize
Bauherr/Client: Ville de Genève
Team: Jean-Paul Jaccaud,
Lionel Spicher, Stephan Gratzer,
Luke Lagier, Marco Ferrari
Fachplaner/Consultants:
T ingénierie SA, SB Techniques SA,
Pierre Buclin SA, MAB ingénierie SA

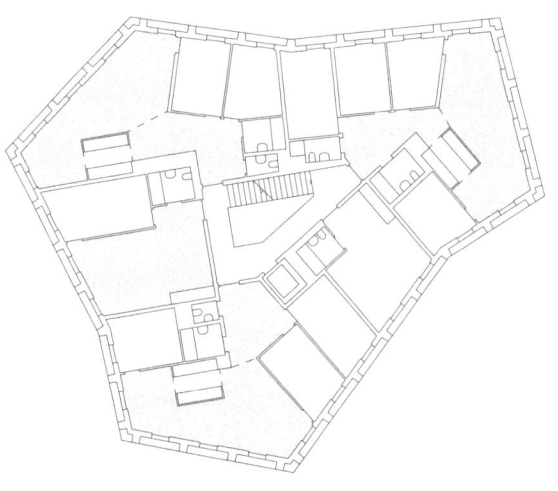

Werkverzeichnis / List of works
Auswahl Bauten, Projekte und Wettbewerbe / Selection of buildings, projects and competitions

2006	Sanierung eines Mehrfamilienhauses, Beirut, Libanon (mit Tanya Zein)
	Haus G, Epalinges S. 32
2007	Renovation einer Wohnung und Fassadensanierung, Chemin du Pommier, Genf
2008	Wettbewerb sozialer Wohnungsbau in la Fontenette, Route de Veyrier, Carouge (2. Preis)
	Wettbewerb Wohnungsbau mit Kinderkrippe, Cologny, Genf
	Wettbewerb Primarschule, Fribourg
2009	Studienauftrag sozialer Wohnungsbau, Avenue Joli-Mont, Genf
	Wettbewerb Wohnungsbau, Avenue de Morges, Lausanne (3. Preis)
2010	Renovation von Büros, Rue de Cornavin, Genf
	Wettbewerb Wohnanlage Les Grottes, Genf (1. Preis) S. 110
2011	Renovation eines Gebäudes an der Albert Street, London (mit Tanya Zein) S. 76
	Wettbewerb Waadtländer Kunstmuseum in Lausanne (mit Sergison Bates architects)
	Wettbewerb Sanierung des Grossratsaales des Kantons Genf (2. Preis)
2012	Sanierung eines Hochhauses mit Wohnungen, Onex, Genf
	Rue du Cendrier Sozialer Wohnungsbau mit Kinderkrippe, Genf (mit Sergison Bates architects; Wettbewerb 2006, 1. Preis) S. 18
	Wettbewerb Wohnanlage, Eaux-Vives, Genf (1. Preis) S. 100
	Wettbewerb Theatersaal, Wohnungen und Büros, Nyon
	Wettbewerb Alters- und Pflegeheim, Vuisternens-devant-Romont (4. Preis)
	Wettbewerb Wohnungs- und Gewerbebauten, Cour de Gare, Sitten (mit Sergison Bates architects)
	Wettbewerb Wohnungs- und Gewerbebauten PAV (La Praille-Acacias-Vernets), Carouge, Genf (mit Sergison Bates architects)
	Wettbewerb Wohnungsbau, Thônex, Genf
2013	Renovation von Musterwohnungen, Quai du Seujet 20, Genf
	Sanierung eines Wohnhauses, Rue du Belvédère, Genf
	Fassaden- und Wohnungssanierung Phase 1, Le Lignon, Genf S. 66
	Wettbewerb Campus HES-SO-EPFL, Sion (mit Sergison Bates architects)
	Wettbewerb Sporthalle, Kinderkrippe und Schule, Sion
	Wettbewerb Sozialer Wohnungsbau, Quartier de La Chapelle, Lancy
	Wettbewerb Sozialer Wohnungsbau, Avenue Henri-Golay, Genf (1. Preis)

2014	Umwandlung eines Industriegebäudes in Saint-Jean, Genf S. 40
	Wettbewerb Secteur Gourgas-Maraîchers, Genf (Studienauftrag, Siegerprojekt)
	Wettbewerb Neuer Sitz der Basler Versicherungen, Basel (eingeladener Wettbewerb)
	Wettbewerb Wohnanlage, Sentier des Saules, Genf (1. Preis) S. 96
	Wettbewerb Sanierung und Aufstockung, Rue de Lausanne, Genf (Studienauftrag, Siegerprojekt)
2015	Sanierung einer Villa, Eaux-Vives, Genf
	Chalet in La Forclaz, Evolène (Jaccaud Zein Architects) S. 56
	Wohnanlage, Shepherdess Walk, London (Jaccaud Zein Architects) S. 82
	Zwei Villen in Chambésy, Genf S. 48
2015	Wettbewerb Universitätsgelände Carouge, Genf (mit Sergison Bates architects, 4. Preis)
	Wettbewerb Wohnungsbau, Quai des Adrets, Genf (mit Sergison Bates architects, 3. Preis)
	Wettbewerb Wohnungsbau, Avenue de Claire-Vue, Genf (1. Preis)
2016	Umbau und Sanierung eines Penthouses, Genf
2016	Wettbewerb Sanierung und Aufstockung, Fondation EPI, Genf (1. Preis)
	Wettbewerb Wohnungsbau für gemeinnützige Wohnbaugenossenschaft, Lancy, Genf (1. Preis)

Laufende Projekte
Sanierung und Aufstockung eines Gebäudes, Rue de Cornavin, Genf
Aufstockung eines Gebäudes, Rue de Beaumont, Genf
Wohnanlage, Eaux-Vives, Genf (Wettbewerb 2012, 1. Preis) S. 100
Sozialer Wohnungsbau, Avenue Henri-Golay, Genf
Wohnanlage, Communaux d'Ambilly, Genf S. 106
Fassaden- und Wohnungssanierung, Le Lignon, Genf S. 66
Sanierung des «kleinen» Turms, Le Lignon, Genf
Secteur Gourgas-Maraîchers, Genf
Wohnanlage, Sentier des Saules, Genf (Wettbewerb 2014, 1. Preis) S. 96
Sanierung und Aufstockung eines Gebäudes, Rue de Lausanne, Genf
Sozialer Wohnungsbau, Avenue de Claire-Vue, Genf
Sanierung, Aufstockung und Neubau von Wohnbauten, Rue de la Servette, Genf
Sanierung und Aufstockung eines Gebäudes, Fondation EPI, Genf
Wohnungsbau für gemeinnützige Wohnbaugenossenschaft, Lancy

Jaccaud Spicher
Architectes Associés

Das Büro wurde 2004 in Genf von Jean-Paul Jaccaud gegründet. Im Jahr 2014 wurde Lionel Spicher zum gleichberechtigten Partner und das Büro wurde in Jaccaud Spicher Architectes Associés umbenannt. Seit 2015 ist Stephan Gratzer Teilhaber des Büros.
Mit seinen Kompetenzen in Architektur, Stadtplanung und Gebäuderenovierung bearbeitet das Büro schweizweit und international Projekte von sehr unterschiedlicher Art und Grösse, von der Aufstellung von Masterplänen über die Errichtung von Wohnungen und öffentlichen Einrichtungen bis hin zur Restaurierung von Gebäuden des modernistischen Erbes. Die Projekte des Büros sind von einem Interesse an kultureller und morphologischer Kontinuität geprägt und suchen nach den jeweils angemessenen Mitteln für präzise, sensible und nachhaltige Lösungen.
Das Büro gewann zahlreiche Preise und Auszeichnungen, darunter 2014 eine Auszeichnung der RIBA für das Gebäude in der Rue du Cendrier in Genf sowie 2012 die Distiction Romande d'Architecture (DRA 3).

Jaccaud Spicher
Architectes Associés

The practice was founded by Jean-Paul Jaccaud in Geneva in 2004. In 2014 Lionel Spicher became a full Partner and the practice was renamed Jaccaud Spicher Architectes Associés. Stephan Gratzer became an Associate in 2015.
With competences in architecture, urbanism and building restoration the practice is involved in projects of different nature and scale in Switzerland and internationally, from masterplanning, housing and public buildings to restoring modernist buildings. The projects of the practice are anchored in an interest for cultural and morphological continuity and consistently look for the adequate means to offer precise, sensitive and sustainable proposals.
The practice has won many awards and prizes, most notably a RIBA award for the building at the Rue du Cendrier in Geneva in 2012 and the Distiction Romande d'Architecture (DRA 3) in 2014.

Partner/Partners	Jean-Paul Jaccaud, Architekt EPF SIA FAS Lionel Spicher, Architekt HES SIA AGA
Teilhaber/Associate	Stephan Gratzer, Dipl. Ing. Architekt TU
Verwaltung/Administration	Michèle Mallet Novelle
Architekten/Architects	Luca Bertolini, Vincent Blanc-Tailleur, Laurent Carrera, Benoît Cousin, Diogo Fonseca Lopes, Giovanna Garbani Nerini, Manon Gerardy, Bastien Guy, Fanny Noël, Magali Michaud, Inês Morão Dias, Baptiste Vaucher
Modellanfertigung / Model maker	Nicolas Schmutz
In Ausbildung / Training	Hillel Marciano, Valentin Chrétien, Amaury Delorme, Isaac Lages Morgado
Ehemalige Mitarbeiter (seit 2004) Former employees (since 2004)	Jonas Altorfer, Valentin Bussard, Frederico Dos Santos, Maxime Duvoisin, Gaëtan Evéquoz, Marco Ferrari, Valérie Galy, Diane Gämperle, Alexandre Hurzeler, Francis Jacquier, Gregor Kamplade, Luke Lagier, Luc Larnaudie, Marlène Leroux, Hildur Ýr Ottósdóttir, Margarethe Mueller, Christophe Neyroud, Vitor Pessoa Colombo, Silvia Palhão, Maryline Perrier, Henriette Ritschel, Anna Salvioni, Christian Schoepp, Gordon Selbach

Jaccaud Zein Architects

Jaccaud Zein Architects wurde 2012 in London als Partnerschaft zwischen Jean-Paul Jaccaud und Tanya Zein gegründet.
Die Arbeit des Büros ist von einem Interesse an Eingriffen in komplexe bauliche Situationen von ausgeprägter Eigenart bestimmt. Alle unsere Projekte schlagen spezifische und sensible Lösungen vor, die vom jeweiligen Kontext ausgehen und besonderen Wert auf die Stimmung und den Wiedererkennungswert des jeweiligen Ortes liegen. Wir glauben entschieden an die Werte des architektonischen und handwerklichen Könnens. Die physischen und emotionalen Eigenschaften der Konstruktion spielen bei allen unseren Projekten eine ebenso wichtige Rolle wie die Materialien mit ihren sinnlichen Eigenschaften, ihrer Patina und ihrer Alterung. Wir haben grosse Erfahrungen in der Errichtung von Wohnbauten und streben kontinuierlich nach Wohnformen, die dem zeitgenössischen Lebensstil entsprechen und Raum lassen für Anpassungen und individuelle Nutzungsformen.

Jaccaud Zein Architects

Jaccaud Zein Architects was founded in 2012 in London as a partnership between Jean-Paul Jaccaud and Tanya Zein.
The practice's work is sustained by an interest for interventions in complex built environments with strong specific identities. All our projects draw on their context to provide sensitive and specific responses and a strong emphasis is put on the definition of atmosphere and the sense of place. We maintain a firm belief in the values of craftsmanship and know-how. The physical and emotional properties of construction play an important part in all projects, as do materials by their sensual properties and their patina and wear. We have an important experience of housing and are constantly seeking residential modes that are adapted to contemporary lifestyle and leave space for adaptation and individuality.

Partner/Partners Jean-Paul Jaccaud, Architekt EPF SIA FAS
Tanya Zein, Architektin EPF SIA FAS RIBA

Architekten/Architects Diogo Fonseca Lopes, Fanny Noël

Jean-Paul Jaccaud

1971	geboren in Hongkong
1991–1992	Aufenthalt in Berlin
1992–1993	Praktikum bei Bernard Huet, Paris
1995	Architekturdiplom an der Ecole Polytechnique Fédérale de Lausanne (EPFL) bei Inès Lamunière und Bernard Huet
1995–1998	Mitarbeit bei David Chipperfield Architects, London
1998–1999	Mitarbeit bei John Mc Aslan & Partners, London
2000–2003	Mitarbeit bei Herzog & de Meuron (London und Basel)
2003	Wissenschaftliche Mitarbeit am Lehrstuhl von Harry Gugger und Christine Binswanger, EPFL
2004	Gründung von Jean-Paul Jaccaud Architectes in Genf
2004–2006	Wissenschaftliche Mitarbeit am Lehrstuhl von Inès Lamunière, EPFL
2006–2010	Gastprofessur an der EPFL
2007–2010	Leitung des Nationalen Forschungprojekts (NFP 54) «Densification des Friches Ferroviaires Urbaines», EPFL
2012	Gründung von Jaccaud Zein Architectes, London, in Partnerschaft mit Tanya Zein Gastprofessur, UCL Löwen, Belgien RIBA-Preis für das Projekt in Rue du Cendrier, Genf
2014	Partnerschaft mit Lionel Spicher und Änderung des Firmennamens von Jean-Paul Jaccaud Architectes zu Jaccaud Spicher Architectes Associés Distinction Romande d'Architecture (DRA 3)
Seit 2015	Mitglied des Bunds Schweizer Architekten (BSA)

1971	Born in Hong Kong
1991–1992	Internship in Berlin
1992–1993	Internship with Bernard Huet, Paris
1995	Architecture diploma at the Federal Institute of Technology Lausanne (EPFL) with Inès Lamunière and Bernard Huet
1995–1998	Collaborator at David Chipperfield Architects, London
1998–1999	Collaborator at John Mc Aslan & Partners, London
2000–2003	Collaborator at Herzog de Meuron (London and Basel)
2003	Assistant to Prof. Harry Gugger and Christine Binswanger, EPFL
2004	Founded Jean-Paul Jaccaud Architects in Geneva
2004–2006	Assistant to Prof. Inès Lamunière, EPFL
2006–2010	Guest Professor at EPFL
2007–2010	Directed the Swiss National Research Projet (PNR 54), "Densification of Disused Railway Areas" at EPFL
2012	Founded Jaccaud Zein Architects in London in partnership with Tanya Zein Guest Professor at the UCL Louvain La Neuve, Belgium RIBA award for the Rue du Cendrier building, Geneva
2014	Partenship with Lionel Spicher. Jean-Paul Jaccaud Architectes renamed Jaccaud Spicher Architectes Associés Received the Distinction Romande d'Architecture (DRA 3)
Since 2015	Member of the Swiss Architects Federation (BSA-FAS)

Lionel Spicher	1978	geboren in Fribourg
	1993–1997	Bauzeichnerlehre
	2002	Architekturdiplom an der Hochschule für Technik und Architektur Fribourg (EIAF)
	2002–2003	Mitarbeit im Atelier Bonnet in Genf
	2004–2007	Mitarbeit bei Pierre-Alain Dupraz Architecte in Genf
	2007	Mitarbeit bei Jean-Paul Jaccaud Architectes in Genf
	Seit 2013	Vorstandsmitglied des Heimatschutzes Genf
		Mitglied der Association Genevoise d'Architectes (AGA)
	2014	Partnerschaft mit Jean-Paul Jaccaud und Änderung des Firmennamens von Jean-Paul Jaccaud Architectes zu Jaccaud Spicher Architectes Associés
	1978	Born in Fribourg
	1993–1997	Apprenticeship as a Technical Draughtsman
	2002	Architecture diploma at the Ecole d'Ingénieurs et d'Architectes de Fribourg (EIAF)
	2002–2003	Collaborator at the Atelier Bonnet in Geneva
	2004–2007	Collaborator at Pierre-Alain Dupraz Architecte in Geneva
	2007	Joined Jean-Paul Jaccaud Architectes in Geneva
	Since 2013	Member of the Committee of Patrimoine Suisse Geneva
		Member of the Association Genevoise d'Architectes (AGA)
	2014	Partnership with Jean-Paul Jaccaud. Jean-Paul Jaccaud Architectes renamed Jaccaud Spicher Architectes Associés
Stephan Gratzer	1982	geboren in Stuttgart
	2006–2009	Mitarbeit bei MGF Architekten – Mahler Günster Fuchs, Stuttgart
	2008	Architekturdiplom an der Universität Stuttgart bei Thomas Jocher und Jan Knippers
	2009	Mitarbeit bei Jean-Paul Jaccaud Architectes in Genf
	2015	Assoziierter Architekt bei Jaccaud Spicher Architectes Associés
	1982	Born in Stuttgart
	2006–2009	Collaborator at MGF Architekten – Mahler Günster Fuchs
	2008	Architecture diploma at the University of Stuttgart in Germany
	2009	Joins Jean-Paul Jaccaud Architectes in Geneva
	2015	Associate archiect at Jaccaud Spicher Architectes Associés
Tanya Zein	1972	geboren in Beirut, Libanon
	1990–1991	Praktikum bei João Luís Carrilho da Graça, Lissabon
	1996	Architekturdiplom an der Ecole Polytechnique Fédérale de Lausanne (EPFL) bei Patrick Berger und Tony Fretton
	1996–2001	Mitarbeit in verschiedenen Architekturbüros in Genf und London
	2001	Gründung von Pfaehler Zein Architectes in Partnerschaft mit Sylvie Pfaehler
	2003	Gründung von L-Architectes in Lausanne in Partnerschaft mit Sylvie Pfaehler und Jeanne Della Casa
	2012	Gründung Jaccaud Zein Architects in London in Partnerschaft mit Jean-Paul Jaccaud
	1972	Born in Beirut, Lebanon
	1990–1991	Internship in Lisbon with João Luís Carrilho da Graça
	1996	Architecture diploma at the Federal Institute of Technology Lausanne (EPFL) with Tony Fretton
	1996–2001	Work experience gained in Geneva and London
	2001	Founded Pfaehler Zein Architectes in partnership with Sylvie Pfaehler
	2003	Founded L-Architectes in Lausanne in partnership with Sylvie Pfaehler and Jeanne Della Casa
	Since 2010	Member of the Swiss Architects Federation (BSA-FAS)
	2012	Founded Jaccaud Zein Architects in London in partneship with Jean-Paul Jaccaud
	Since 2015	Member of the Central Committee of the Swiss Architects Federation (BSA-FAS)

Bibliografie / Bibliography	2002	Jean-Paul Jaccaud / Blaise Sahy: Kaserne Basel – Atelier Binswanger, Gugger, Jaccaud, Sahy. Lausanne.
	2004	Jean-Paul Jaccaud: Une œuvre presque inachevée. La foire internationale de Tripoli au Liban. In: Faces Nr. 56, S. 58–61.
	2006	Habiter la Menace – ouvrage collectif sous la direction d'Inès Lamunière. Lausanne. Rue du Cendrier 1–3. In: Publications Ville de Genève. Genf. Tony Fretton: Grand Angle, maison à Epalinges, Vaud. In: Faces Nr. 63, S. 48–52. Jean-Paul Jaccaud / Nadja Maillard: Huit petites pièces. In: Espaces Contemporains Nr. 2, S. 53–92.
	2007	Nadja Maillard: Une pente, un pli. In: Espaces Contemporains Nr. 5, S. 108–112. Martin Steinmann: Sommerlich. In: Werk, Bauen + Wohnen Nr. 1/2, S. 56–58.
	2008	Jean-Paul Jaccaud / Vincent Kaufmann: Friches ferroviaires urbaines en Suisse: un potentiel à conquérir. In: Journal Le Temps, 8. November, S. 17.
	2009	Densification des friches ferroviaires Urbaines (Band 1 und 2). Lausanne.
	2011	Jean-Paul Jaccaud: Symbolic atrophies. In: Revista NU Nr. 37, S. 36–42. Ellis Woodman: Geneva Accord. In: Building Design Nr. 1996, S. 10–15.
	2012	Feeling at Home. In: 13th International Architecture Exhibitions at the Venice Biennale (Ausstellungskatalog). Pergine Valsugana, S. 46–51. Jean-Paul Jaccaud: Localising Architecture. In: Revista NU Nr. 38, April, S. 26–29. Diogo Lopes: Jean-Paul Jaccaud. In: Revista NU Nr. 38, April, S. 42–51. Martin Steinmann: Eine eigene raison d'être. In: Werk, Bauen + Wohnen, März, S. 34–41.
	2013	La rue des Cordiers – La complexité en second plan. In: Interface 17. Genf, S. 24–25. Anna Hohler: Voisinages urbains. In: Tracés Nr. 11, S. 7–12. Jean-Paul Jaccaud – Proximités et résonances, le projet de Cour de Gare à Sion. In: Tracés Nr. 18, S. 10–11. Jean-Paul Jaccaud: Life Class. In: Building Design Nr. 2053. London, März. La rue des Cordiers – La complexité en second plan. In: Interface 17. Genf, S. 24–25. Anna Hohler: Voisinages urbains. In: Tracés Nr. 11, S. 7–12. Steffen Hägele: Sir Robin, Wohnüberbauung und Krippe, Genf. In: Architese Nr. 1, S. 38–41. Hugh Strange: Le Lignon Apartment Complex. In: Building Design Nr. 2057.
	2014	Distinction Romande d'Architecture. In: Catalogue de la DRA 3. Lausanne, S. 11. Lorette Coen: Une décennie d'Architecture. In: Espaces Contemporains Nr. 2, S. 114–119.
	2015	Ellie Duffy: Home is where the House is. In: UN Cube Magazine online, 22. Dezember.
	2016	Residential Complex London. In: Domus Nr. 998, S. 62–73. Grégoire Farquet: La différence. In: Hochparterre Wettbewerbe Nr. 1, S. 38–41. Edwin Heathcote: New Vernacular Brickism. In: Financial Times, 20. Februar, S. 10–11. Jan-Carlos Kucharek: Shepheress Walk Housing. In: RIBA Journal, Januar, S. 34–36. Rown Moore: New Kid on the Block. In: The Observer, 7. Februar, S. 30. Daniel Rosbottom: Artful Ambiguity. In: ORIS Nr. 99, S. 80–89. Deborah Saunt: Corner to Corner. In: Architecture Today Nr. 264, S. 44–53. Ellis Woodman: Building Study Shepherdess Walk. In: The Architects Journal Nr. 243, S. 32–45.

Textbeitrag / Article by	Irina Davidovici wurde in Bukarest, Rumänien, geboren. Sie absolvierte ihr Architekturstudium in London und arbeitete in den Büros von Caruso St. John und Herzog & de Meuron, bevor sie an der Universität Cambridge in Geschichte und Philosophie promovierte. Sie schreibt regelmässig Beiträge für internationale Publikationen, die sich durch eine Verschmelzung architektonischer Geschichte, Praxis und Kritik auszeichnen. Die Tatsache, dass sie sowohl Architekturtheoretikerin als auch praktizierende Architektin ist, ist eine gute Basis für einen konstruktiven Dialog zwischen Architektur als Konstruktion und geschichtlichem Hintergrund. Davidovici ist leitende Dozentin für Geschichte und Theorie der Architektur an der Kingston University in London und Autorin von *Forms of Practice: German-Swiss Architecture 1980–2000* (Zürich, 2012).

Dank

Mein herzlicher Dank gilt Linus, Heinz und Antonia Wirz für ihre Begeisterung, ihre Unterstützung und ihre Geduld bei der Vorbereitung dieser Publikation. Wegen der Belastung durch die Leitung der Büros, durch laufende Projekte und notwendige Reisen war ich leider nicht immer verfügbar und daher danke ich von ganzem Herzen für das grosszügige Verständnis, das sie meiner «elastischen» Auslegung von Terminabsprachen entgegenbrachten.

Mein Dank gilt ausserdem Irina Davidovici, der Freundin und regelmässigen Diskussionspartnerin, die unser Anliegen so deutlich erfasst und unsere Diskussionen auf sensible und verständnisvolle Art festgehalten hat.

Ein Dank gebührt auch allen unseren Partnern, Kunden und den Unternehmen, die durch ihre grosszügige Unterstützung zu diesem Buch beigetragen haben, insbesondere Yannos Ioannides, Gilles et Yves Aknin, Paul Epiney, Isabelle Charollais, Philippe Meylan, Pierre Alain l'Hôte und José Manuel Campos. Herzlichen Dank auch an Volker Trommsdorff, Jörg Koch, Roger und Gus Zogolovitch für ihre Freundschaft, ihre Unterstützung und ihr langjähriges Vertrauen.

Weiterhin danke ich den Mitarbeitern Rui Agnelo und Benoît Cousin, die an der Vorbereitung des Buchs mitgewirkt haben, sowie Noémie Gygax für ihre ausgezeichnete grafische Arbeit und ihre Geduld.

Und zum Schluss möchte ich noch meinen Büropartnern Lionel Spicher, Tanya Zein und Stephan Gratzer für ihre ausserordentliche Gestaltungsfantasie, ihre Diskussionsbeiträge, ihre Kritik, ihre Sympathie und ihre Grossherzigkeit danken. Ohne sie wären die in diesem Buch vorgestellten Projekte niemals zustande gekommen.

Acknowledgements

I would like to thank wholeheartedly Linus, Heinz and Antonia Wirz for their enthusiasm, their support and their patience in the elaboration of this publication. Between managing offices and projects and travelling my availability has not been obvious and I would like to thank them for their generosity and understanding with my rather elastic approach to deadlines.

Many thanks also to Irina Davidovici, friend and regular discussion partner, for steering our conversation so accurately and re-transcribing it with such sensitivity.

Thank you to all our partners, clients and contractors who so generously contributed to this publication, particularly Yannos Ioannides, Gilles and Yves Aknin, Paul Epiney, Isabelle Charollais, Philippe Meylan, Pierre Alain l'Hôte and José Manuel Campos. Many thanks also to Volker Trommsdorff, Jörg Koch and Roger and Gus Zogolovitch for their friendship and their unwavering support over the years.

Thank you to the collaborators who prepared this book, Rui Agnelo and Benoît Cousin and to Noémie Gygax for her excellent work as graphic designer and for her patience.

A special thank you to my partners, Lionel Spicher, Tanya Zein and Stephan Gratzer for their extraordinary capacity for design, discussion, critique, sympathy and generosity. Without them none of the work in this book would exist.

Jean-Paul Jaccaud 2016

C 21
Comptoir d'Investissements
Immobiliers SA, Sitten

Batima (Suisse) SA, Genf

Prelco,
Préfabrication d'éléments
de construction SA, Genf

Seical SARL, Genf

Quart Verlag Luzern / Quart Publishers Lucerne

De aedibus – Zeitgenössische Architekten und ihre Bauten / Contemporary architects and their buildings

62	Jean-Paul Jaccaud (de/en und de/fr)	31	Neff Neumann (de/en)
61	huggenbergerfries (de/en)	30	Giraudi Wettstein (de/en)
60	Berrel Berrel Kräutler (de/en)	29	Steinmann & Schmid (de/en)
59	Pierre-Alain Dupraz (de/en und de/fr)	28	Matthias Ackermann (de/en)
58	Cometti Truffer (de/en)	27	Aeby & Perneger (de/en)
57	Joos & Mathys (de/en)	26	Bakker & Blanc (de/en)
56	Lacroix Chessex (de/en)	25	Markus Wespi Jérôme de Meuron (de/en)
55	Savioz Fabrizzi (de/en und de/fr)	24	Bauart (de/en und de/fr)
54	Boegli Kramp (de/en)	23	Knapkiewicz & Fickert (de/en)
53	Zita Cotti (de/en)	22	Marcel Ferrier (de/en)
52	Oestreich + Schmid (de/en)	21	Wild Bär Architekten (de/en)
51	Stump & Schibli Architekten (de/en)	20	Enzmann + Fischer (de/en)
50	Luca Gazzaniga (de/en)	19	Mierta und Kurt Lazzarini (de/en)
49	Guignard & Saner (de/en)	18	Rolf Mühlethaler (de/en)
48	Morger + Dettli (de/en)	17	Pablo Horváth (de/en)
47	Charles Pictet (de/en)	16	Brauen + Wälchli (de/en)
46	Armando Ruinelli + Partner (de/en/it)	15	E2A Eckert Eckert Architekten (de/en)
45	Luca Selva Architekten (de/en)	14	Lussi + Halter (de/en)
44	Luca Deon (de/en)	13	Philipp Brühwiler (de/en)
43	2b (de/en)	12	Scheitlin – Syfrig + Partner (de/en)
42	Durisch + Nolli (de/en)	11	Vittorio Magnago Lampugnani (de/en)
41	sabarchitekten (de/en)	10	Bonnard Woeffray (de/en und de/fr)
40	Beat Rothen (de/en)	9	Graber Pulver (de/en)
39	Atelier Bonnet (de/en)	8	Burkhalter Sumi / Makiol Wiederkehr (de/en)
38	Novaron (de/en)	7	Gigon/Guyer (de und en)
37	Althammer Hochuli (de/en)	6	Andrea Bassi (de, fr und en)
36	Schneider & Schneider (de/en)	5	Dieter Jüngling und Andreas Hagmann (de und en)
35	Frei & Ehrensperger (de und en)	4	Beat Consoni (de und en)
34	Liechti Graf Zumsteg (de/en)	3	Max Bosshard & Christoph Luchsinger (de)
33	Adrian Streich (de/en)	2	Miroslav Šik (de, en und it)
32	Daniele Marques (de/en)	1	Valentin Bearth & Andrea Deplazes (de, en und it)

Quart Verlag GmbH, Heinz Wirz; Verlag für Architektur und Kunst
Denkmalstrasse 2, CH-6006 Luzern; books@quart.ch, www.quart.ch